BOON
ASHES

David Boon
Ken Davis

The laughs, legends, matches, captains, selectors, mates, jokes, yarns, tours, sixes, teams, family, stats, stories, umpires.

Published by:
Wilkinson Publishing Pty Ltd
ACN 006 042 173
Level 4, 2 Collins Street
Melbourne, Vic 3000
Ph: 03 9654 5446

National Library of Australia Cataloguing-in-Publication data:

Boon, David, 1960- .
Boony's Ashes : the laughs, legends, matches, captains, selectors, mates, jokes, yarns, tours, sixes, teams, family, stories, umpires.

ISBN 0 9775457 2 5.

1. Boon, David, 1960- . 2. Test matches (Cricket) - Anecdotes. 3. Cricket players - Biography. I. Davis, Ken, 1948- . II. Title.

796.35865092

Cover and page design: Michael Bannenberg
Illustrator: Paul Harvey
Printed in Australia by McPherson's Printing Group, Maryborough, Victoria

Dedication

This book is dedicated book to my children Georgie, Jack and Lizzie who give me so much joy and of whom I am so proud.

Without surprise, I especially enjoy supporting them as they play their chosen sports and try to be the best they can be.

David Boon.

The Authors

David Boon, like Slim Dusty's hat and Phar Lap's heart is a national treasure. Sure he averaged almost 44 in 107 Tests but this gritty right hander's value to our nation goes well beyond some jumble of numbers and decimal points.

Dubbed the "Keg on Legs" Boon won the hearts and minds of all Australians with his pugnacious playing style and popular larrikin streak. Not only the best batsman on the planet, he was seen as the best bloke too.

A fighter, a cult hero, a legend.

"Cricketers can be respected and even deeply respected," ABC commentator Neville Oliver wrote. "But David Boon... he was a player they loved."

Boon was the Bulldog of the Aussie batting line up. A gladiator who enjoyed going toe-to-toe with Sir Richard Hadlee and Caribbean killers Michael Holding and Curtly Ambrose – revelling in the challenge of leading Australia's assault from the top three.

It was this warrior instinct that saw Boon standing on a Jamaican pitch in 1991 blood oozing from a large cut under his chin as team physio Errol Alcott pleaded– unsuccessfully – for him to leave the field. But the bloodied batsman refused to break. Refused, even, to rub the spot.

And so with scrappy pieces of white plaster stuck to his bearded chin, Boon batted out the 15 remaining minutes until lunch – then casually walked from the field to receive six stitches without anaesthetic.

The plucky Australian number three rejoined the battle after the break too ... finishing his innings unbeaten on 109.

Nick Walshaw, *Australian Cricket*

Ken Davis wrote about cricket for a number of newspapers in Australia for more than 20 years. Additionally he has been communications advisor to Cricket Victoria, Cricket Australia and the International Cricket Council.

He was married the night before the Centenary Test so he would have somewhere to go on his honeymoon and skilfully managed the birth of his son so that he did not miss the first match under lights at the MCG in 1985.

Today he runs his own public relations company and remains involved in journalism and cricket.

Surprisingly he is still married to Sally, the bride from the Centenary Test. They have two children.

The authors, David Boon, cricketer extraordinaire, and Ken Davis, cricket tragic, would like to thank Ken Williams for his assistance. Surely one of the game's finest archivists, his accurate knowledge of facts, figures, who, when and how is peppered throughout this publication.

CHAPTERS

in retaining them and becoming part of the most powerful team in the world.

The Australian selector settles down to pick his greatest Australian side and a Rest of the World team to play it.
Mind games and controversy for the cricket fan or to discuss with the bloke at the bar.

SUMMER OF THE BOONY DOLL

During a One-Day match in Sydney last summer I wandered onto the SCG for a presentation. I was just a bit player in the proceedings but suddenly this cry of "Boony, Boony" erupted around the ground.

From the other officials with me came a few smiles and the odd look of disbelief. In the media area there were some scathing comments. Richie Benaud correctly said: "Wasn't that popular when he played."

I was just embarrassed and would have loved to have disappeared down a hole if there had been one nearby.

ABC radio described the response as even warmer than when "Barbie found her Ken doll."

"It's the summer of the Boony Doll."

Indeed it was.

A few months earlier I had been sitting in my Hobart office in the winter of 2005 looking at the snow on Mt Wellington and ruminating over the Ashes battle in England when I received a phone call from a marketing representative of Foster's.

The brewery was already a strong supporter of Australian cricket and especially of Tasmanian cricket through their Cascade brand.

The brewery was looking for summer promotion and had come across the technology that could be inserted into a small figurine and would react with unique signals sent out through a television broadcast.

The brewery had researched their adult market and also their target 18–25-year-old to find a unique player who was popular with the fans and had unique physical attributes that would allow for the manufacture of a small figurine that was instantly and easily recognised.

Left: Hitting the winning runs to win the Ashes at Old Trafford 1989. *Graham Morris Photography*

Merv with the moustache? Gilchrist with the gloves? Taylor with the tub? What about Lillee in full flight? No. They wanted the bandy legged little Boon.

I was flabbergasted. Overwhelmed. Remembered after a decade away from the Test arena.

A doll that looked like me, sat on top of the television and commented on the cricket. I was rather hesitant about whether it would be a success. Who would want me in their lounge room chatting to them during the cricket? Don't think I would!

Anyway a quick check with my employers, the Tasmanian and Australian cricket authorities, and the Boony Doll was born.

The designer of the figurine put a few pounds on the fella to make him more "cuddly." In fact Boony started to look a bit like "little Merv" until we settled on the girth!

It went onto the market as a VB promotion and suddenly the Boony Doll was a star.

Boonanza

By Philip Derriman, *Sydney Morning Herald*, December 10, 2005

DAVID Boon's elevation to icon status can be traced to the early 1990s when Rob Sitch and Santo Cilauro made him the subject of a regular skit on ABC Television's The Late Show. *"Boony" was their idol. They'd face Launceston, his home town, drop to their knees and chant, "Legend, legend, deadset legend ... top bloke."*

At the time it wasn't entirely clear why Boon was singled out for the attention. He'd always been a rather dour character on the field, who took his cricket seriously and never played to the crowd. Hardly the stuff personalities are made of.

Photo courtesy Foster's Australia

Yet, like Doug Walters before him, who was just as subdued, Boon obviously appealed in a special way to ordinary punters, so much so that, at 44, he's back featuring in VB beer's TV promotion. In one commercial he stands in a glass case alongside Phar Lap's glass case in the Melbourne Museum, which is probably as iconic as you can get. Boon was really there in a case, too – it's not a computerised imagery.

VB has 200,000 electronic Boony dolls on offer. If you watch the coming one-dayers against South Africa and Sri Lanka with a Boony doll beside you, it will speak to you periodically, triggered by audio signals via Channel Nine's telecast. All up, the doll has 37 different things to say, but it's not Boon's voice you will hear. That was judged to be too low and gravelly. Somebody who sounds like Boon but projects better supplied the speech.

VB's ad agency, George Patterson Y & R, didn't set out to build the promotion around Boon. The starting point was the technology that enables the dolls to talk. Initially, the idea was to have a talking bat or ball. Then an inspired agency person, who may have watched The Late Show *all those years ago, said, "Why not have a talking Boony?"*

George Patterson Y & R's promotion manager, Iain Crittenden, says it wasn't hard to persuade Boon to be part of the campaign. What's the secret of his appeal? "He's enigmatic, a bit larger than life," Crittenden said. "For people enjoying the cricket and a beer, he's someone they can relate to."

The doll was a roaring success. Over 200,000 dolls were purchased through the promotion which was the most successful ever conducted by the brewery. And of course the Boony Doll is back again for this Ashes tour – accompanied by some retired English cricketer! Boony Dolls were sent around the world as presents and as travelling companions for

back packing Aussies.

The Boony Doll even has his own blog site on the web and he has been photographed visiting the Eiffel Tower, the leaning tower of Pisa and even high in the Andes.

He sat in the Speaker's chair at Parliament House in Canberra and for two hours chatted about his life as a doll and sporting icon with an announcer on Rockhampton radio. I missed the broadcast but a couple of interstate truck drivers who were in the vicinity claim it was the weirdest piece of radio they had ever heard during their travels around Australia

The little fella is only supposed to react to Network Nine cricket commentaries but we first heard of a small technical glitch when he started asking for nachos, "I like Nachos," while watching soccer on television in a bar in Mexico!

Boony look-a-likes, 2005. *Photo courtesy Foster's Australia*

Well it might be the moustache. He looks a bit Mexican.

At the end of the summer and the close of the cricket season the Boony Doll was supposed to become mute. A silent sentinel left in the corner of the lounge room to become dusty and forgotten.

But the little bloke hadn't read the script. In May he began

to speak again – around the world. Was the cricket on? It was time for a beer, and as for those damn Nachos ... !

The phone calls started. A mate of mine, Roscoe Barrett of Albion Cricket Helmets returned to his holiday house after a couple of hours on the beach to find his Italian mother-in-law sitting outside in a lather of perspiration which he thought was caused by the heat.

"Roscoe, Roscoe you must sell this house. It is haunted. There is a ghost in there asking for someone to go to the fridge for a beer. I am too afraid to go back inside."

I had a box in my office with about 50 of the little fellas which I was giving away during the summer. Late one night they all started talking again which frightened the hell out of the cricket secretary at the Tasmanian Cricket Association.

Even the Boon household was not saved. Every Sunday morning the little fella would ask for some Nachos or ask someone to get him a beer. Unfortunately he was in my daughter's room and woke up the entire house ... except for me!

After three Sunday performances he was consigned to the shed. The family was sick of him and abused me!

Another started chatting on a Qantas flight, another at a bank in the middle of the night setting off an alarm. In Dubai at the headquarters of the International Cricket Council he asked for a beer during a world wide teleconference.

It was all to do with the battery running down and at first it was funny but then some people, not necessarily the dolls' owners, became a little disgruntled. Especially if the owner was absent.

In the *New York Times*, where many Australian journalists and frustrated cricket fans reside, a reporter on assignment in South America came back to find his doll in pieces on his desk. An accompanying unsigned note said: "Your little mate

7

was driving me mad. Also I have never understood cricket, it's boring." An unsportsmanlike act from a colleague!

At the United Nations' headquarters in New York, Boony was a wandering vagrant. He mysteriously moved from office to office overnight. Naturally when he started talking again it started a number of international incidents – especially among international delegates who didn't understand cricket or Australian humour!

But possibly the finest story about a born again Boony Doll comes from just across the road from Buckingham Palace where the "Queen's Guard" is domiciled.

A Boony Doll was put in a locker and forgotten by one of the guardsmen. He began talking during an inspection of quarters by the Sergeant-Major. Obviously a man without a sense of humour, he placed the six members of the dormitory on report until they confessed as to who had been talking behind his back and imitating his Scottish voice!

Of course when the doll was found he refused to say a thing. Their "confined to barracks" remained in place and the "Curse of the Bonny Doll" had hit London!

Boony's Shout–The Motor Mouth won't go away

By Bridie Smith, *The Age*, May 9, 2006

BOONY is mouthing off again. Months after the VB cricket series ended, the promotional talking Boony Doll is at it once more.

"When are we going to the pub?" has woken many Australians as the figurine came out of hibernation and just had to sound off.

Foster's Australia spokeswoman Felicity Watson said the doll's unprompted "expert comments" – programmed to be uttered only during the VB one-day series – were being reported in Victoria, Western Australia and Queensland.

"I think he's been acting a little bit like an alarm clock for some people too," she admitted. "We were surprised to hear such widespread stories of him coming back to life for a second time."

She said Foster's Australia believed Boony – inspired by former Australian batsman David Boon – had come back to life, thanks to a battery more powerful than expected.

"It looks like some batteries have had a little bit more life in them, and some Boonys have gone back into their talking phase," she said.

Owners of the digital technology, the American-based Veil Technology, which also supplies Mattel and Warner Bros with interactive technology, are investigating. Ms Watson said people should not try to remove the battery, but should move the doll out of earshot.

"I wouldn't want to encourage people to tinker with it, and people can rest assured, he can't talk forever," she said.

The doll was programmed to respond to electronic triggers aired during television coverage of the cricket.

More than 200,000 dolls were given away with slabs of VB during the summer promotion.

They became among the most traded items on eBay in January, when almost 2000 were listed.

The highest bid was $222.50, while the average price was $24.05.

Foster's Australia reported their best beer sales in a decade in half-year results released in February, with little doubt the spike was helped by the Boony Doll and promotion.

Boony look-a-likes, 2005. *Photo courtesy Foster's Australia*

COMIC
CRICKET COMMENTATORS

Just love them. I didn't realise how funny they were until I retired. It's easy to make a mistake. That's why I avoid the microphone.

My old team mate Dean Jones fled Sri Lanka in disgrace in August after describing a Muslim cricketer as a terrorist in an on-air gaffe that was immediately branded racist. "The terrorist has got another wicket," he said when South African Hashim Amia, a devout Muslim, took a catch.

Certainly Deano thought the microphone was off and he was sitting at the back of the commentary box. But he left his brain in neutral and his mouth in overdrive.

But it's easy to do. Just try these gaffes, tongue twisters and meaningless meanders for size.

"Cowdrey in slip. Legs wide apart, waiting for the tickle."
John Arlott, BBC Radio

"Statistics are like short skirts. What they reveal is always suggestive."
Kerry O'Keeffe, ABC Radio

"Very small crowd here today. I can count them on one hand. Only about 30 spectators."
Graham Dawson, ABC Radio

"An accurate bowler. He hits the middle of the bat every time."
Drew Morphett, ABC Radio

"Laird has been brought in to stand in the corner of the circle."
Richie Benaud, Nine Network
"That was a tremendous six; the ball was still in the air as it went

over the boundary."
Fred Trueman, BBC Radio

"Anyone foolish enough to predict the outcome of this match is a fool."
Fred Trueman, BBC Radio

"Unless something happens that we can't predict, I don't think a lot will happen."
Fred Trueman, BBC Radio

"On the first day, Gus Logie decided to chance his arm and it came off."
Trevor Bailey, BBC Radio

"We don't have service or servants like that in England."
David Gower, Nine Network, after watching a cute blonde bikini-clad Aussie queue up repeatedly for beers for four male friends at the Adelaide Oval in 1989

"There's a fielding epidemic going around ... and it's NOT catching!"
Robin Jackman on BBC after a number of catches had been dropped

"Batsman's Holding, the bowler's Willey."
Brian Johnston, BBC Radio

Richard Hadlee and Richie Benaud were commentating. Michael Atherton was hit in the box and Hadlee said:
"That ball bounced."
Benaud replied with:
"Which one?"

Brian Lara had been hit in the box by Steve Waugh and on BBC Television, David Gower said:

"Brian Lara faces Steve Waugh ... one ball left."

"Greg Chappell at first slip wearing the long sleeved jumper, wide brim hat and long sleeved shirt. Ian Chappell at second slip wearing a short sleeved jumper and wide brim hat and Redpath at third slip wearing no jumper at all ... sort of like a progressive strip tease!"
John Arlott, BBC Radio

"There was a slight interruption there for athletics."
Richie Benaud, BBC Television, when a streaker ran across the field

"Wickets are like wives, you never know which way they will turn."
Kerry O'Keeffe, ABC Radio

"Mike Gatting now has a fine leg – that's a contradiction in terms."
Richie Benaud, Nine Network

"Michael Clarke reminds me of that pop star, what's his name? Oh yes, it's effineff,"
said David Lloyd
"David, its eminem, I think,"
replied David Gower, BBC Radio

"It's been very slow and dull day, but it hasn't been boring. It's been a good, entertaining day's cricket."
Tony Benneworth, ABC Radio

"It is important for England to take wickets if they are going to make big inroads into this Australian batting line-up."
Max Walker, Nine Network

"What's your favourite animal, Steve?"
"Merv Hughes."

Steve Waugh being interviewed by the Comedy Show

Tossing the haggis in the Highland Games in Scotland in 1989. *Photo Graham Morris.*

IT'S A FUNNY GAME

Cricket has made me laugh a million times – and not just at Merv Hughes trying to tongue kiss fieldsmen's ears. Perhaps it's because we spend so many hours in the field that anything appears funny. Here are a few memories:

Allan Border

"I am not talking to anyone in the British media ... they are all pricks."
Allan Border, Australia's captain at our press conference at Hove in 1993

"Hey, hey, hey, hey! I'm f***ing talking to you. Come here, come here. Do that again and you're on the next plane home. What was that? You f***ing test me and you'll see."
Border in a mid-pitch exchange with Craig McDermott at Taunton in 1993. McDermott had asked to bowl at the other end

"What do you think this is, a f***ing tea party? No you can't have a f***ing glass of water. You can f***ing wait like all the rest of us."
Allan Border, getting tough with England batsman Robin Smith at the Trent Bridge Test during the 1989 tour

We were out celebrating a win over the Poms in Perth and late at night AB decided to peel off and go back to the hotel.

Walked up to the desk at the Sheraton: "The key to room 544 if you please"

"I am sorry sir you cannot have it!"

"Of course I can have it. I have been staying here for six days and we are not leaving until tomorrow. Key to 544 please." The skipper was adamant.

"I am sorry sir. You may be staying in room 544 and you

may be staying in Perth, but not at this hotel. You are staying at the Hyatt!"

Fat Cat

Undoubtedly Queenslander Greg Ritchie missed his calling in life and should have been an explosions expert in the army. He was never without penny bungers and other assorted fireworks and crackers.

For some reason he found a long-standing victim in Adelaide cricket writer Alan Sheill.

In India we were all having a beer in the gardens of our hotel and feeling a bit bored one evening between matches. Nicknamed "Fat Cat" because he was cuddly, Ritchie had been missing for a while and when he returned he crept along on all fours up behind Sheill, who was lounging back in his chair sucking on a beer as usual. Ritchie planted a giant cracker under him with a very long fuse.

Then he lit the fuse, crawled away and moments later came sauntering around the corner and joined in the conversation. We watched in awe as the fuse burnt slowly.

Boom!!!

Sheill jumped a metre in the air in absolute terror and then started after the Fat Cat who was away like lightning. But Ritchie was great at escaping from his angry targets.

"That's it I'm off bed you bunch of silly b......s".

We resumed pleasantries, Greg Ritchie warily returned and then for the next 10 minutes all was back to normal.

Then another giant explosion from one of the bedrooms overlooking the bar and pool. I don't know how he did it but the Fat Cat had set another much larger firecracker in Sheill's room with a slow burning, long delay fuse.

Suddenly Sheill was on his balcony in his pyjamas and hurling abuse at Ritchie while we rolled around laughing.

"I'll get you Ritchie. You are a menace to society. You are bloody mad!"

After that every one on the tour kept looking behind them and scoured their room for firecrackers before they headed off to bed.

Rolling Stone

In 1989 at Lord's my mother spent a few hours sitting beside "quite a nice man with long hair." She never recognised Mick Jagger. He came into the rooms after the match and spoke about sitting beside a very nice woman who knew quite a bit about cricket. He didn't recognise my mother.

ABC Average

Bradman's final Test average of 99.94 is commemorated in the ABC's postal address in Australia. In each state and territory it is – PO Box 9994.

Steve Waugh

"With the possible exception of Rolf Harris, no other Australian has inflicted more pain and grief on Englishmen since Don Bradman." *The Daily Mirror's*, Mike Walters, on Steve Waugh's retirement.

Shane Warne

"How anyone can spin a ball the width of Gatting boggles the mind."
Martin Johnson, in *The Independent*, on Shane Warne's ball of the century which bowled Mike Gatting in 1993.

Bowlers

"McCague will go down in Test cricket history as the rat that joined the sinking ship."
Daily Telegraph Mirror in Sydney upon Martin McCague's 1993 selection for England against Australia, where he was raised and schooled.

Bodyline

"Don't give the bastard a drink. Let him die of thirst." An Australian supporter's advice, in Sydney, to the 12th men when they were taking drinks to the players while Jardine was batting in the Bodyline series, 1932-33.

"A cricket tour in Australia would be the most delightful period in your life ... if you were deaf."
Harold Larwood, England's main fast bowler on the Bodyline tour. He later emigrated to Australia.

"All Australians are an uneducated and unruly mob."
Douglas Jardine to Stork Hendry, Australia's wicket-keeper, during the Bodyline series.

"Well, we shall win the Ashes but we may lose a Dominion." Rockley Wilson, former first-class cricketer and Douglas Jardine's coach at Winchester on hearing that Jardine would captain MCC in Australia, 1932-33.

Tuffers

"Phil Tufnell! Can I borrow your brain? I'm building an idiot."
One of the funnier Australian barrackers, Ashes, 1994-95.

Thommo

"I dunno. Maybe it's that tally-ho lads attitude. You know, there'll always be an England, all that Empire crap they dish out.

But I never could cop Poms."
Jeff Thomson, Australian fast bowler, 1987.

England

"All the never-say-die qualities of a kamikaze pilot."
England's cricketers in the 1990s, as seen by an Australian
journalist.

Character Reference

"If you're playing against the Australians, you don't walk."
Ian Botham, in court during Imran Khan libel action, 1996.
Not walking had been suggested as an example of unreliable
character.

Can we quote you?

"England has only three major problems. They can't bat,
they can't bowl and they can't field." Martin Johnson's famed
assessment in *The Independent* at the start of England's tour of
Australia 1986-87. England's recovery to win the Ashes later led
Johnson to remark: "Right quote; wrong team."

David Gower

Always wore red socks when fielding and blue when
batting.

Viv Richards

Richards is probably the only batsman to be out for a
duck on three occasions in a match. This incident is described
in his biography. Richards was a hero in Antigua and the entire
island had come to St. John's Park to watch a Red Stripe game
and see their man in action.

Antigua batted first and the entire crowd exploded when

their favourite son stepped out to bat.

First ball, Richards nicked a catch to the keeper. The umpire had no difficulty with the decision and a disappointed Richards made his way slowly back to the dressing room. But he didn't reach it. The crowd, stunned by losing their entertainment went wild and the umpire, fearing for his life, changed his decision.

Reluctantly, Richards came back. Not for long. Soon he was dismissed again and the umpire, in a surge of bravado gave him out again. This time he ignored the crowd.

Richards, however, had more disappointment – the second time around he made another duck!

Umpire

Just before a match at the MCG, the secretary of Cricket Victoria, Ken Jacobs, received a message that Bill Smyth, (the world's oldest living Test umpire,) was at the turnstile with two friends and was chasing some spare tickets.

"Throw him out. He is an impostor. Whoever heard of an umpire with two friends?"

Tragic

Journalist Ken Davis, who helped me write this book, is a cricket "tragic."

He was married the night before the Centenary Test in 1977. "I wanted somewhere interesting to go for my honeymoon. My wife went home to her mother."

Then eight years later and about to become parents he had his wife induced so that he could be at the MCG for the first match under lights.

"Would have liked to bring the little fellow with me but the wife wouldn't allow it."

Merv was very dutiful at breakfast, lunch and dinner but Errol was watching him like a hawk.

The afternoon tea at the MCG in those days was a silver service affair straight from the members' dining room with party pies, pastie slices, sandwiches and at the end of the table some fruit and a tiny salad.

About half an hour after the tea break Errol came into the room. "Where is Merv?"

Much shaking of heads and muttering "Don't know."

Errol's suspicions were aroused and he quickly headed off to the afternoon tea room. No sign of Merv and the left-over food had been cleaned away.

Indoor nets? No. Back in the room he visited the toilet and noticed a cubicle was being occupied. Quietly pulling up a chair he looked over the top of the door.

There was Merv with a silver tray on his knees finishing off the left-over pies and sandwiches. On the floor beside him was a giant two litre bottle of coke!

Laying on the rub down table after another Herculean performance with the ball. "My foot, ankle and knee are telling my stomach to stop eating." There was a pause.

"My stomach is telling my foot, ankle and knee to stop whining and get on with the job."

Ricky Ponting

His debut for Tasmania was as a teenager in Adelaide. Bad habits from home arrived with him. First morning he slept in, missed breakfast and barely made the bus in time.

Mark Waugh

I scored 40 century partnerships in Test cricket. Remarkably

11 of them with Mark Waugh – undoubtedly Australia's most elegant batsman. Talk about Beauty and the Beast!

Geoff Marsh

Before every Test match we always had a players' dinner at which coach Bob Simpson would run through the game plan and then Allan Border would discuss the opposition and how we could exploit any weaknesses.

Traditionally after he finished he would look across at his vice captain Geoff Marsh: "Anything to add, Swampy?"

"No, you have covered it all," was the inevitable response.

But before the First Test in Brisbane when asked by the skipper he said, "Yes."

We were astounded. You could have heard a pin drop and we all suddenly craned forward to hear what surely would be memorable words from the West Australian farmer.

"Gentleman, we are playing against the West Indies, the best cricket team in the world. We can win if we make enough runs and then get them out for less runs. But in order to get those runs we know we are going to get hit and we are going to get hurt. But we cannot show them that we have been hurt."

Then sat down. We were amazed. We had waited more than 50 Tests for that?

The next morning AB won the toss. There had been a storm overnight and the wicket had a strong tinge of green. Ideal conditions for bowling.

Our skipper decided to bat. So Geoff Marsh and I headed out to open the innings.

First over from Malcolm Marshall and no one was hit, second over from Patrick Patterson same again. Third over from Marshall and still not a bruise. Next over Patterson broke down

and they threw the ball to a tall gangly bloke who had been wandering around the outfield.

The two openers had a chat.

"Good to see Patterson off."

"Know much about this bloke?"

"Nay."

"Cannot possibly be as quick as the other two!"

I went back to face the new fellow as fieldsmen gathered around me. The new bowler was Curtly Ambrose and his first ball rocketed into my ribs!

I had tears in my eyes as Ambrose glared at me, waiting for a response. But I remembered what Swampy Marsh had said the previous night. I stared back at Curtly until he turned around a headed back to his mark.

At that stage my inspirational vice captain walked down from his place of safety beside the umpire. "Babs, you can give it a little rub if you want!"

Patrick Patterson

Just before the close of the fourth day's play at the Melbourne Test against the West Indies in 1988-89, Patrick Patterson was batting when there was a stumping appeal against him. Given out he argued that his foot was on the line. AB gave him both barrels, politely explaining the law and making reference to the mentality of fast bowlers.

At stumps Patterson raged into the Australian dressing room and promised to kill us all out in the middle the next day. He didn't quite manage that. In a frenzied spell of 5/39, he came bloody close.

Dean Jones

Australia was going along quite nicely in a World Series

Final against the West Indies until Dean Jones asked Curtly Ambrose to remove his white wristband, believing it was camouflaging the white ball and distracting the batsmen.

Thanks Dean. Ambrose took off his wristband then tore through Australia taking 5/32 including Dean's wicket quite cheaply.

Tony Greig

At the start of England's 1974-75 tour of Australia, Tony Greig obviously decided to try and get into Dennis Lillee's head.

First he bounced him out, which prompted Lillee to storm back into the Australian dressing room and announce, "Just remember who started this thing, we will finish it."

Then Greig, while making a brilliant 110 in the first innings at Brisbane treated Lillee, who had just come back after a serious back injury, like a dog constantly goading him: "That's four, go and fetch it," and cockily shadow boxing his bouncers. It was one of Greig's finest innings as he drove and sliced Lillee and Jeff Thomson over slips with arrogance to continue his love/hate relationship with the Australian team and Australian fans.

I am happy to report Australia had the last laugh winning the series 4-1.

Room Mates

Everyone asks about big Merv Hughes whenever you mention room mates.

"How bad was he?" they ask.

Tremendous. One of the best. Always made me a cup of tea in the morning and could lift anyone's spirits if they were down in the dumps.

He looked a fright. Completely covered in hair like a gorilla.

Shocking sight to look at first thing in the morning!

Among the others:

Geoff Lawson, an educated professional man. An optometrist who would spray lavender oil around the room and light scented candles. Not your normal fast bowler.

Geoff Marsh, just the opposite. A farmer from out of the back of beyond in Western Australia. If it hadn't been for me guiding him he would have been perpetually lost. Big cities bewildered and baffled him.

Greg Matthews was different but a fantastic cricketer. Rooming with him was a new experience. He would like to "air his body" in the room and some of his nocturnal habits were non-traditional. Let's leave it there.

Steve Waugh, untidy. Surely he cannot be like it at home. Clothes and kit all over the room.

Undoubtedly the worst was a fellow Tasmanian. Mark Atkinson was like a tornado. His room was a disaster. And tight! He used to take his own washing powder around with him to do his washing. Then would sell it to his team mates at 50 cents a handful. He did get better.

Duchess of Norfolk

First match of my first Ashes tour was against the Duchess of Norfolk's XI at the beautiful Arundel castle. It was bizarre. The hosts were short of players. We had plenty so I started my tour playing for an English team!

It was freezing. Always is, and I made 34.

Next tour in 1989 I made sure I played for Australia and scored 134. In the picnic atmosphere of the match Allan Border hit a huge 6 which broke a woman's nose.

Two for openers in Brisbane in 1991 before the first Test against India. *J. Barnes Photography*

Away on tour the player with the best jokes is always popular – gets invited out to dinner a lot more than anyone else. I love a good joke and a good joke teller.

My favourite joke of all time which I heard in a pub in Launceston.

The Expectant Father

An expectant father rang the hospital to see how his wife was getting on. In his excitement he rang the MCG. "How's it going?" he asked. "Fine," came the answer, "we've got three out and hope to have the rest out before lunch. The last one was a duck."

A Magnificent Spud

A famous cricketer was invited to Penguin on the north coast of Tasmania to play against local farmers. He walked onto the field to tremendous applause from the crowd. He took guard and faced the local fast bowler. The first ball uprooted his stumps. As he walked out he called to the bowler, "Magnificent ball." "What did you expect," the bowler growled, "a bloody potato?"

Smart As

In a local district match in Melbourne the umpire was being jeered and heckled unmercifully from the crowd. At tea he walked over to the boundary and sat down next to his chief critic. "What are you doing?" asked the spectator. "Well," said the umpire, "it seems you get the best view from here."

A Slip Fieldsman

A slip fieldsman had a particularly black day in a match in Mackay in Queensland during which he dropped no less than six

catches, all off the same bowler. After the game he was talking to the bowler when he broke off and looked at his watch. "I must go," he said, "I have a bus to catch." The bowler looked at him bitterly. "Let's hope you have better luck with that, then."

Need an Umpire?

In England the village teams were ready to begin their match but discovered that they didn't have an umpire. They decided that they would use a member of the crowd even though he didn't know the rules. When he was dressed in his white coat and hat, he went up to the captain of the home side.

"What do I do?" he asked.

"It's very simple," said the captain. "When I shout, HOWZAT! you simply put up your finger and say OUT. When it's our turn to bat, I'll tell thee a little bit more!"

LBW

During a match in Lithgow in the Blue Mountains, the fieldsman positioned just behind the umpire kept trying to distract the batsman. Several appeals for LBW were turned down, and finally the umpire turned to the fieldsman and said sternly: "I've been watching you for the last 10 minutes."

"I thought so; I could tell you weren't watching the game!"

Catch?

Down Sale way in Victoria, someone asked the local club's president, "Tell me, is your daughter's fiancé a good catch?" "Good catch? He's the best fielder we've got in the side!"

Liars

Two old cricketers were talking in the club.

"What was your highest score?"

"A hundred and ten not out."

"Mine was a hundred and twenty not out."

"And what was the most number of wickets you took?"

"Oh, no. This time you go first."

Psychiatric Help

The cricketer was visiting the psychiatrist.

Cricketer: "It's terrible. I can't score runs, I'm a terrible bowler, and I can't hold a catch. What can I do?"

Doctor: "Get another job."

Cricketer: "I can't. I'm playing for England tomorrow!"

Walk?

The batsman received a fast ball which struck his pad. Though it was obviously LBW he danced around and fell to the ground clutching his foot. The umpire came rushing up. "Can you walk?" he asked.

"Barely."

"Then walk back to the pavilion, you're out."

Cricket Explained

You have two sides one out in the field and one in. Each man that's in the side that's in goes out and when he's out, he comes in and the next man goes in until he's out.

When they are all out, the side that's out comes in and the side that's been in goes out and tries to get those coming in, out.

Sometimes you get men still in and not out.

When both sides have been in and out including the not outs, that's the end of the game!

Howzat!!!

Lord

An Earl was batting in a village match and his butler was

the umpire. A local bowled and plainly caught the lord, LBW. He appealed to the butler who said, "Lord Peterson is not at home." "What?" said the Earl. "Well, your lordship," said the butler, "to speak plainly, you're out."

Deano

"It's amazing," Dean Jones told his Victorian team mates after returning from England, "there I was at Lord's, when suddenly about 100 people crowded round me all waving autograph books!"

"Come off it, Deano."

"It's true. If you don't believe me ask David Gower he was standing right next to me!"

New Wife

The young new wife of a suburban cricketer went to the local sports store. "I'd like a hundred runs, please."

"A hundred runs?" the salesman asked.

"Yes, for my husband's birthday," she said, "it's something he said he has always wanted!"

New Team Mate

The new fieldsman had a high opinion of himself and was very free with his advice to the captain.

"You know," he said, "you've got two players who should never be in the side."

"Oh really," said the captain icily, "and who's the other one?"

Keeper Quiet

In a grade cricket in Sydney a young batsman was having a terrible time at the crease. He stammered to the wicket-keeper, "Well, I expect you've seen worse players?" Silence ... He said, "I

said, I expect you've seen worse players?"

"I heard you the first time. I was just trying to think."

Out!

Over in Perth in a suburban game, the batsman was out first ball. "Not like last week," said the wicket-keeper.

"No," said the batsman. "Last week I stayed in and got 40 and when I got back all the beer was gone!"

Hopeless

"You're looking sad."

"Yes, my doctor says I can't play cricket."

"Really! I didn't know he'd ever seen you play!"

Awful

The two rival cricketers were talking. "The local team wants me to play for them very badly."

"Well, you're just the man for the job."

Lord's 1989, a quiet comment with Mike Gatting.

It's been happening for generations.

Just ask any former player. It happened in the Bodyline series. We used it to try and break the batsman's concentration. Under Steve Waugh it was used to virtually disintegrate the confidence of the opposition.

I loved it.

Under the helmet and in my favourite bat pad position which was within touching distance of the batsman, I could say what I liked without the umpires hearing a thing.

But you had to pick your target. You never sledged New Zealand's John Wright, he fed off it.

But sledging can be subtle. South African Darryl Cullinan was Shane Warne's "bunny" and was all at sea against him.

On one occasion when he was taking block against him I whispered from bat pad, "I'm here to help you."

He didn't say a word. Didn't even look at me.

"The first ball will be a small leg break, so soft hands and just play it away." It was and he did.

"Do you trust me?" I asked. He smiled.

"Next will be a big leggie and Warnie often drags it down so you should cut it for four through that gap at point and get off the mark."

It was the big leggie. He let it go. "Idiot!" I said. "But do you trust me now?"

He smiled again.

"Next will be the top spinner so come forward with nice soft hands and you will be fine." He did.

"Do you trust me now?" He almost laughed.

"Okay Darrell, here comes the flipper, now for God's sake

37

no matter what you see out of the hand GO FORWARD."

He went back, lbw Warne 0.

He muttered something and then trudged off yet again.

It took a couple of years but Cullinan got his revenge on Warne (but not me!). The South African was on his way to the wicket and Shane Warne warmly greeted his bunny and told him he had been waiting two years for another chance to humiliate him.

"Looks like you spent it eating," Cullinan retorted.

Malcolm Marshall was bowling to me and I had played and missed a couple of times. "Now David, are you going to get out now or am I going to have to bowl around the wicket and kill you?" Funny now, but frightening at the time.

Fred Trueman was bowling when the batsman edged and the ball to first slip and between the Rev. David Sheppard's legs. Fred didn't say a word. At the end of the over, Sheppard (later England captain and also Bishop of Liverpool) ambled past Trueman and apologised: "I should've kept my legs together, Fred."

"So should your mother," was the reply

When Ian Botham took guard in an Ashes match, Rod Marsh welcomed him to the wicket with the immortal words: "So how's your wife and my kids?"

Rod went on to manage elite cricket programs for youths in

Australia and England. Wonder what he taught them?

Shane Warne, trying to tempt a young South African batsman out of his crease asked what it took to get the tubby chap to come forward. I was having a fairly lazy day at short leg as wicket-keeper Ian Healy piped up: "Put a Mars Bar just short of a good length. That should do it."

The batsman's quick response, "You had better make it two in case Boony gets there before me."

Ian Healy's legendary comment was picked up by the Channel 9 microphones when Arjuna Ranatunga called for a runner on a particularly hot night during a one dayer in Sydney. "You don't get a runner for being an overweight, unfit, fat prick!"

During a test match in the West Indies, Merv Hughes didn't say a word to Viv Richards, but continued to stare at him after each delivery. Richards responded: "This is my island, my culture. Don't you be staring at me. In my culture we just bowl." Merv didn't reply, but after he dismissed him he announced to the batsman: "In my culture we just say piss off."

During the 1991 Adelaide Test, Javed Miandad called Merv a bus conductor. A few balls later Merv dismissed Javed: "Tickets please," Merv called out as he ran past the departing batsman.

During the 1989 Lord's Test, Merv Hughes said to Robin Smith after he played and missed: "You can't f***ing bat."

Smith replied to Hughes after he smacked him to the boundary, "Hey Merv, we make a fine pair. I can't f***ing bat and you can't f***ing bowl."

BAT PAD SPECIALIST

I made a name for myself in the unique and ridiculous forward short leg position. I developed the idea in conjunction with coach Bob Simpson. I felt that a looming fielding presence in the corner of the batsman's view would be unsettling. I must have been an idiot because from that day bat pad became a specialist position. But not that stupid as I had substantially reduced the number of times I had to chase the leather around the outfield.

The best of times

I loved fielding in the batsman's hip pocket. Certainly better than or having to wait under a sky ball while every spectator and television camera concentrated on your nervousness under the descending ball.

At bat pad, apart from offering the occasional piece of advice on batting technique, I was always in the game.

The most memorable?

Shane Warne's Hat Trick

My 34th birthday was the final morning of the Second Ashes Test at the MCG. Australia was already one up in the series due to Mark Waugh and Michael Slater centuries, along with Shane Warne taking 8-71 in the second innings in Brisbane. The match was meandering without a boundary in the first hour and Alec Stewart doggedly holding the team together.

Then Warne struck. He trapped Phil DeFreitas lbw, then next ball Darren Gough edged to Ian Healy behind the stumps. Two wickets in two balls. Was a hat trick in the wind?

Shane went back to his mark and started babbling to his fellow Victorian Damien Fleming at mid-off. He had been the

last Aussie to take a hat trick and tried to offer some sensible advice. But Shane kept asking, "What am I going to bowl? What will I bowl?"

Fleming quickly lost interest as everything he said was being ignored. "Just bowl anything!"

Shane decided on the top spinner to Devon Malcolm believing that if he spun it too far the English tailender would swing and miss. So Shane bowled, it "kicked" when it bounced as the batsman prodded forward. The ball caught his glove and ballooned in the air.

Normally you want the ball to come to you. But when it's a hat trick? What if you drop it! Please not me.

But there was no one else. I threw myself at the ball and the fingers scraped soil as a couple slipped under the quickly descending ball. Just got it! Then I was up and pumping with jubilation. Then, just as suddenly, Shane was all over me. He had sprinted the fastest I had ever seen him move. What an honour!

Allan Lamb

The opening Ashes Test of 1989; Terry Alderman was as tight and deadly as usual. The Englishman played an ungainly shot and the ball rocketed high to my right. Snapped it up.

Sanjay Manjrekar

Merv Hughes took the first four wickets and I caught three of them at the wicket. The others had been reflex catches but with this one I seemed to have all the time in the world and took it with both hands. Looks great on replay and yet another instance of me assisting Merv Hughes' cricket career.

Mohammad Azharuddin

Some dismissals are even planned. So it was at the SCG in 1992 when Allan Border and I decided I would stand a metre deeper as Azharuddin was a fluent shot maker. Sure enough Craig McDermott bowled a slower ball. He was early into the shot and hit it like a tracer bullet. In a reflex action I stopped it with one hand and dived backwards to complete the catch before I hit the ground.

Brian Lara

Another piece of planning. In Antigua in 1995 Steve Waugh was bowling his extremely useful medium pacers on a slow wicket. He reckoned that by bowling continually at off stump, and even wider, a frustrated Lara would try and lift one over to leg. He moved me to close mid-on and sure enough two overs later it came high hard and looping to my left. Who would have thought that the little fella could get that far off the ground without a trampoline?

And the worst

Of course at bat pad you can get in the way, literally. On the 1989 tour I was belted twice in the same week. Against Nottinghamshire that pesky little Derek Randall of Centenary Test fame, was bouncing all over the crease like a deranged

puppet. Usually you can get an idea where the ball is going by the positioning of the feet – as well as watching the ball off the bat, but not with Derek.

Carl Rackeman tried to bounce him and Randall swung around and pulled him straight towards my face. It was straight into the front of the grill. I disappeared into never-never land for a few minutes.

Would you believe a week later it was the Fifth Test and Robin Smith, one of the hardest hitting batsmen in the game, was facing Trevor Hohns, a leg spinner who later made his name as Australian Chairman of Selectors.

My helmet was in for repairs following the previous week's experience and I had borrowed Carl Rackeman's, which was one of the original designs with the grill attached to the earpieces.

I saw the foot planted, the bat swing, knew I was in strife and turned my head. It hit me side on and the entire helmet shattered. Smith thought he killed me, I felt all-right apart from an ache in my right forehead. When I went to speak my entire jaw clicked back into place!

A few minutes later I was off the ground and resting with a huge headache looming. After the day's play Dean Jones wandered into in the rooms. "This must be yours."

He had found a fragment of the helmet outside the boundary rope and between overs had paced it out. Exactly 100 paces from where I was hit.

Suddenly the headache was worse. In fact it was a dislocation, which miraculously had slipped back into place.

The term "Ashes" was first used after England lost to Australia – for the first time on home soil – at The Oval in 1882. *The Sporting Times* carried a mock obituary to English cricket which concluded that, "The body will be cremated and the ashes taken to Australia."

Fred Spofforth – "The Demon" – took 14 English wickets for 90 and was largely responsible for the famous victory. After a dreadful start with the tourists all out for 63 runs in the first innings William Murdoch's men recovered their composure to seal victory narrowly by some seven runs inside two days! The breathless tension of the final innings with Spofforth overwhelming the England batsmen is the sort of thing that leads to legends and none more so than this epic encounter.

One spectator suffered a heart attack. Another ate through the handle of his umbrella!

The following Saturday the famous mock obituary for English cricket appeared – an epitaph that lingers to this day and ensures posterity for the author.

In Affectionate Remembrance

of

ENGLISH CRICKET,

which died at The Oval

on

29th AUGUST, 1882,

Deeply lamented by a large circle of sorrowing friends and

acquaintances

R.I.P.

N.B. – *The body will be cremated and the ashes taken to Australia.*

Left: Sydney Test, Australia vs England 1990-1.
Gregg Porteous Photography

It was left to the Hon. Ivo Bligh to retrieve English honour the following Australian summer. The First Test at Melbourne and the Fourth at Sydney were lost but the Second and Third at Melbourne and Sydney were won by Bligh's men and so honour was restored!

During their stay in Melbourne, Bligh's party stayed at Rupertwood – the country home in Sunbury of William Clarke. It was here that the Ashes itself became a reality.

A game was played between the tourists and a number of others on the Clarke paddock. Unfortunately there remains some doubt as to whether the actual ashes were the remains of the ball used in that game or the bails. Whichever, these ashes were presented to Bligh by the ladies of the household which included Florence Morphy.

Florence was the music teacher to the Clarke family and a companion to Sir William Clarke's wife, Lady Janet.

The final game of the 1882-83 tour was against Victoria at Melbourne in March and in the post match banquet there was much talk of the "Ashes" by both Bligh and the Chairman of the Melbourne Cricket Club, F. G. Smith. Shortly after this game Bligh sailed for England.

Bligh returned to Australia later in 1883 to marry Florence Morphy. In 1888 the married couple returned to England. Bligh's father, the 6th Earl Darnley, died in 1896 and the eldest son, Edward Bligh succeeded him. But Ivo became the eighth Earl Darnley in 1900 on the death of his brother, and settled in the family home of Cobham Hall.

The Earl died in 1927 and two years later Dame Florence gave the Ashes to Lord's.

More than 75 years on, the tiny, delicate and irreplaceable urn remains in the MCC Museum at Lord's.

After discussions with the England & Wales Cricket Board

(ECB) and Cricket Australia, MCC commissioned an Ashes-shaped Waterford trophy, which was first presented to Mark Taylor after his Australian side emerged triumphant in the 1998-99 Test series against England.

Since then, this crystal trophy has been presented to the winning captain at the end of each Test series between Australia and England.

Footnote: The Lord Protector of England, Oliver Cromwell banned the playing of "Krickett" in Ireland by an order of 1656. All "sticks and balls" were henceforth to be burnt (and thereby reduced to ashes!) by the common hangman.

The Ashes urn © MCC/Terry Murphy Photography

101 Facts You Didn't Know about the Ashes

I love digging around for offbeat cricket facts and stories about the Ashes. Like most people I have probably forgotten more than I remember. But here are a few for your next cricket trivial pursuit night.

Early Years

The first Test match was played at the Melbourne Cricket Ground in March 1877, between a combined Victorian and New South Wales XI and an all-professional English side led by James Lillywhite Jnr, a 35-year-old left-arm bowler from Sussex. Australia ran out winners by 45 runs, but in the return match a fortnight later England was victorious by four wickets.

Australia's first Test captain was Dave Gregory, a 31-year-old all-rounder from NSW. In a short Test career, he led Australia in the first three Tests and on the 1878 tour of England (during which no Tests were played).

The first Test began just one day after the Englishmen had returned to Australia, after a rough voyage across the Tasman Sea and from an arduous six-week tour of New Zealand.

Gloveman Gaoled

They came back without the services of wicket-keeper, Edward Pooley.

No stranger to trouble, Pooley had been arrested following an incident in a Christchurch hotel and was forced to remain in New Zealand awaiting trial on charges of assault and damage to property. He was eventually acquitted, but missed the Test matches in Australia and never represented his country again.

Left: Post bat pad catch Australia v New Zealand. A typical Merv Hughes assault, please leave me alone!
Gregg Porteous Photography

First Out

The first player to be dismissed in Test cricket was Nat Thomson, Charles Bannerman's 37-year-old opening partner, who was bowled for one by Allen Hill in the fourth over. Hill, a fast bowler from Yorkshire, also held the first catch in Test cricket, when he caught Tom Horan from the bowling of Alfred Shaw.

First Century

On the opening day, Bannerman took full advantage of some loose bowling and fielding to record the first Test century. At stumps, after three and a quarter hour's batting, he had scored 126 out of Australia's total of 6 for 166.

Next day he took his score to 165 when, with the score on 7 for 240, a lifting delivery from George Ulyett split open the middle finger of his right hand. The wound required stitching and he was unable to resume.

Bannerman was responsible for 67.34% of Australia's completed total of 245, which remains the oldest record in Test cricket. The closest it has come to being beaten was in January 1999, when Michael Slater (123) made 66.84% of Australia's runs in its second innings of 184 in the Fifth Test against England at Sydney.

Bannerman's 165 remains the highest score by an Australian on his Test debut, although several players, Archie Jackson (164 v. England 1928-29) Kepler Wessels (162 v. England 1982-83), Wayne B Phillips (159 v. Pakistan 1983-84) and Doug Walters (155 v. England 1965-66) have come close to beating it.

Remarkably, Bannerman played in only two more Tests (although he later umpired 12 Tests) and his 165 was his only century in first class cricket. During his long career for NSW, from 1870-71 to 1887-88, his highest score was 83.

Youngest Ever

The second highest score in Australia's first innings was 18 not out by Tom Garrett. Garrett was just 18 years and 232 days of age on the opening day of the match and he remains the youngest player from either country to appear in Ashes Tests. A lively medium paced bowler and hard hitting lower order batsman, he played in another 17 Tests and represented NSW until 1897-98.

Foot in Both Camps

The first five wicket haul in Test cricket was taken by Billy Midwinter, who captured 5/78 from 54 four ball overs in England's first innings of 196. A fine all rounder, Midwinter has the unique distinction of playing for both countries in the Ashes Tests. Born in England, he came to Australia at the age of nine and made his first class debut for Victoria in 1874-75.

He departed for England straight after the first two Tests, and represented Gloucestershire, the county of his birth, for six seasons, during which time he played four Tests for England as a member of Alfred Shaw's team that toured Australia in 1881-82. After returning to Australia in late 1882, he played a further six Tests for Australia. He died in 1890 at the age of 39, becoming the first Australian Test cricketer to die.

Midwinter is not the only man to play Tests for and against Australia, Kepler Wessels played 24 Tests for Australia from 1982-83 to 1985-86, and later captained South Africa in five Tests against Australia in 1993-4.

Tom Who?

Australia's bowling star of the first Test was Tom Kendall, a left handed medium pacer from Victoria, who captured 7/55 in England's second innings after it had been set 154 to win.

Remarkably Kendall was making his first class debut and appeared in only one more Test.

International Flavour

Only five members of the first Australian side – Nat Thomson, Dave Gregory and his elder brother Ned, Jack Blackham and Tom Garrett – were locally born. Four – Charles Bannerman, Billy Midwinter, Tom Kendall and Jack Hodges – were born in England, while Tom Horan was born in County Cork, Ireland and Bransby Cooper in Dacca, India (now Dhaka, Bangladesh).

Gregory Dynasty

Dave and Ned Gregory who were the first brothers to play Test cricket, belonged to a remarkable cricketing family. Two other brothers played for NSW, while Ned's son Syd played 58 Tests for Australia, and another son, Charles, played for NSW. Jack Gregory, Australia's outstanding all-rounder of the 1920s, was Dave and Ned's nephew.

Ned Gregory, who later became curator at the SCG, has the dubious distinction of recording the first duck in Test cricket. He made 11 in the second innings, but he and Bransby Cooper, who made 15 and 3, were both dropped for the Second Test and never played Test cricket again.

Oldest

James Southerton, a slow right-hand round arm bowler from Surrey, who was 49 years and 119 days old on the opening day of the First Test, remains the oldest Test debutant from any country. He died in June 1880, becoming the first Test cricketer to die.

The oldest player to appear in an Ashes Test was Australia's Bert Ironmonger, who was 50 years and 327 days on the

Right: After winning One-Day Series in West Indies, 1991. *Gregg Porteous Photography*

Botham & Border's
ASHES CLASHES

35 Years of Ashes Action -
The Inside Story

ALL ACTION CRICKET
OVER 3 HOURS

G

AVAILABLE NOW ON DVD

Botham & Border's
ASHES
CLASHES

Join cricketing legends Ian Botham and Allan Border for their own exclusive review of thirty-five thrilling years of The Ashes.

Over three hours long - and packed with the very best action from all nineteen series played in Australia and England between 1970 and 2005 - *Ashes Clashes* brings together these giants of the game once again.

There is no rivalry in sport greater than that between Australia and England at cricket – but now Botham and Border team up to give the inside story of thirty-five action-packed years.

No-one knows the Ashes better. Botham, one of England's all-time great swashbuckling heroes, dominated Ashes Tests between 1977 and 1989. Border, one of Australia's most successful captains and batsmen, joined the fray in 1978, bowing out in 1993. The two became the best of enemies - totally committed on the field, friends for life off it.

Now join them for an unrivalled insight into the joy and heartache that goes into winning and losing The Ashes. Relive the very best of the last thirty-five years of Ashes series – the years of Lillee and Thomson; Gower and Gatting; Warne and McGrath; Flintoff and Vaughan … and, of course, Botham and Border.

final day of the Fifth Test of the Bodyline series in 1932-33. At the time Ironmonger, a slow left-arm bowler from Victoria, was believed to have been 45 or 46 years of age and it was not until his death at the age of 89 in 1971, that his birth certificate was uncovered, which revealed that he had been born in 1882.

W. G. Grace was exactly a week younger on the last day of his final Test appearance for England, at Trent Bridge in 1899.

Demon

The first ten wicket haul in Test cricket was achieved by Fred "Demon" Spofforth in the one-off Test at Melbourne in 1878-79. He took 6/48 and 7/62 and recorded the first hat trick in Test cricket, when he dismissed Vernon Royle, Francis MacKinnon and Tom Emmett with successive deliveries in the first innings.

MacKinnon, who later became the 35th head of the MacKinnon clan, made only 0 and 5 in his sole Test, but has the distinction of being the longest-lived Test cricketer to date, surviving to the age of 98 years and 234 days.

Lord's, Graces and Death

Although Lord's is now regarded as the traditional "home" of cricket, it did not stage its first Test until 1884. The first Test in England was played at Kennington Oval in London in September 1880.

The England side for the match included three Graces, the only instance of three brothers appearing together in the same side in an Ashes Test. "W.G." made 152, England's first Test century and shared an opening stand of 91 with his elder brother "E.M" who made 36.

The third brother, G. F. "Fred" Grace was dismissed for a "pair," but took a remarkable outfield catch to dismiss the

Australian big-hitter George Bonnor. The batsmen had almost completed their third run by the time Grace took the catch and afterwards he claimed that his heart stopped beating while waiting for the ball to descend. Perhaps it did – he died from pneumonia only a fortnight later.

First Skipper's Century

Billy Murdoch who succeeded Dave Gregory as Australia's captain for the 1880 tour, became the first Australian captain to make a Test century when he made 153 not out in Australia's second innings. His great innings could not save Australia from defeat, however, after it had followed on 271 runs in arrears. Murdoch went on to captain three more Australian sides to England, in 1882, 1884 and 1890.

Long Time Between Draws

The 1881-82 English team to Australia was the first of four teams brought out to Australia in the 1880s as business ventures by the partnership of professional cricketers James Lillywhite, Alfred Shaw and Arthur Shrewsbury. The side, which was captained by Shaw and included the Australian, Billy Midwinter, played two Tests in Melbourne and two in Sydney, the first to be held there.

Australia won both Tests in Sydney but the two in Melbourne were drawn. Subsequently, all Tests in Australia until the Second World War were played to a finish, so that the next drawn Ashes Test in Australia occurred 64 years later.

Hat Tricks

Billy Bates recorded England's first Test hat trick in the Second Test at Melbourne in 1882 when he dismissed Percy McDonnell, George Giffen and George Bonnor with successive

57

balls in Australia's first innings.

His match figures of 14/102 remained an England record for over 20 years. An excellent all-rounder from Yorkshire, Bates' cricket career came to a sudden end on the same ground in five years time when he lost the sight of an eye after being accidentally struck by a ball at net practice.

Bowlers Please

The entire English side bowled during the first innings of the Third Test at The Oval in 1884 with the wicket-keeper Hon. Alfred Lyttleton, with underarm lobs, taking the bowling honours with 4/19. Remarkably these were the only wickets he took during his 101-match first-class career.

In reply, England made 346 to save the game, with Walter Read top-scoring with 117 batting at number 10. Furious at being sent in so late, he reached his hundred in under two hours and put on 151 for the ninth wicket with Walter Scotton, which is still England's record partnership for that wicket against Australia.

Australia's Reggie Duff (in 1901-02) is the only other player to make an Ashes hundred batting at number 10.

Out

In 1884 the entire Australian team refused to play in the Second Test at Melbourne after the authorities refused their demand for 50 per cent of the gate money.

As a result an entirely new team took the field of whom only Tommy Horan, who was made captain, and Sammy Jones had previously played Test cricket. Of the nine newcomers, five made their only Test appearance in this game. The weakened Australian team lost by nine wickets.

Among the newcomers making their only Test appearance was Sam Morris, whose parents had migrated to Australia from

Cricketer as Tough as Teak *by Ken Davis*

Whenever the name David Boon is mentioned the adjectives flow and the admiration mounts like the runs from his bat.

Pugnacious, tough as teak, tough as old rope, tenacious, the beating heart of Australian cricket. Prime Minister John Howard referred to him as a National Icon.

All these terms rained down when the squat Tasmanian surprised cricket fans across the world when he pulled stumps on his Test innings.

The battle-scarred Allan Border, who seemed to spend his career rescuing Australia from tortuous positions, said that if you were to pick someone to bat for your life then he would always nominate the tough little Tasmanian. David Boon served his State and his nation with enormous distinction.

As a teenager he was a hero of Tasmania's historic initial win of the One-Day series in 1978-79, played a vital role in four Ashes Series wins, was Man of the Match as Australia turned the cricket world on its ear and initiated an awe-inspiring epoch in the 1987 World Cup Final.

In his home town of Launceston they named a grandstand after him while he was still in his twenties and only in mid-career. Following his retirement they named November 14, 1996 as David Boon Day and an all star testimonial match was held in his honour.

David Boon's father Clarrie was a highly respected sports administrator. His mother Lesley played hockey for Australia when barely out of her teens. At Launceston Grammar Boon excelled at cricket, football and especially swimming.

Then Lancashire professional Jack Simmons arrived in Tasmania to lead the island state into the national One-Day competition and eventually Shield cricket. He nominated that

Boon would one day play for Australia, nurtured and guided his career and selected him as a teenager in one of the initial Tasmanian One-Day teams.

Boon and his wife Pip recognised the friendship and respect by naming their son after him.

Gillette Cup Semi-final, Brisbane 1978. In the dressing room with Jack Simmons my coach/captain after I hit the winning four.

Boon's efforts on his three tours of England reflected his career. In 1985 he scored heavily in the County games but seemed anchored to the crease against the spin of John Emburey and his seven innings produced only 124 runs at 17.7. In 1989 he returned a complete batsman to score 442 runs at 55.25 but lived in the shadow of Steve Waugh and Mark Taylor who feasted on the English offerings.

In 1993 he was one of the most assured batsmen in the world. His concentration was legendary and his shot selection almost faultless. His patience was copybook. He defended the good ball, any short ball was cut for four, and if the ball was overpitched clipped away through mid wicket.

Where previously he scored invaluable cameo half centuries now he determinedly sought higher honours. His 10 Test innings averaged 69.37 and he finally achieved his ambition of reaching three figures in England. Following a frustrating 93 in the First Test at Old Trafford he followed up with a century at Lord's.

A century at the home of cricket. He humbly stood in the company of cricket greats.

Then another in the Third Test and then the Fourth Test. He had equalled Sir Donald Bradman's legendary three in a row! By the end of his career he had played in 107 Tests for Australia, scored 7,422 runs which put him among the game's higher echelon of Australian batsmen and finished with an average of 43.65.

He was Man of the Match in the 1987 World Cup Final and from 1989 batted at number three for his nation, following in the footsteps of Bradman and exhibiting many of the same stoic characteristics.

He finished his career with a first class average of 46.01, averaged 62.72 in England, 68 in India, scored 15 centuries in Australia and the same number while touring.

Barbados during the gold rushes, making him the first Test cricketer of West Indian descent.

Born to Rule

Tom Horan, born at Midleton, County Cork, Ireland, is one of only two Australian captains not to be born in Australia – the other being Percy McDonell (London).

By contrast 12 players who have captained England in Ashes Tests were born outside England – Lord Harris (St. Anne's, Trinidad), "Plum" Warner (Port of Spain, Trinidad), Frederick Fane (Curragh Camp, Ireland), Douglas Jardine (Bombay, India), Cyril Walters (Bedlinog, Wales), 'Gubby' Allen (Sydney, Australia), Freddie Brown (Lima, Peru), Colin Cowdrey (Bangalore, India), Ted Dexter (Milan, Italy), Mike Denness (Bellshill, Scotland), Tony Greig (Queenstown, South Africa) and Nasser Hussain (Madras, India).

Two Into One

Inter-colonial rivalry resulted in two England sides touring Australia simultaneously in 1887-88. One was invited by the NSW Cricket Association and was led by C. Aubrey Smith, a left-arm bowler from Sussex, who later became a famous Hollywood movie actor.

The other was organised by the Hon. Martin Hawke, at the invitation of the Melbourne Cricket Club. As Hawke had to leave for home early, following the death of his father, the team was led by G. F. Vernon, by whose name the team is generally known. Both teams suffered heavy financial losses.

The rival teams pooled their players for a one-off Test at Sydney under the captaincy of Walter Read late in the season. England won by 126 runs and Australia's first innings of 42 (George Lohmann 5/17 and Bobby Peel 5/18) remains its lowest

Test score in Australia. Fewer than 2000 spectators attended the three days of play making it the worst attended Ashes Test of all time.

Quick Cricket

All three Tests of the 1888 series in England were completed inside three days. Australia won the First, at Lord's, to record its first Test victory in England since its triumph at The Oval in 1882, but lost the remaining two by an innings.

An extraordinary feature of the 1888 tour was the bowling of Charlie 'the Terror' Turner (right-arm medium fast) and Jack Ferris (slow left-arm) who between them captured 482 wickets in first-class matches (Turner 283 and Ferris 199).

Selectors' Mistakes Back in 1890

Even in those days selectors made mistakes. The 1890 Australian side to England included Kenny Burn, the first Tasmanian to play Test cricket. In arguably the biggest selection bungle of all time, Burn was chosen as the team's second wicket-keeper, but when he joined his team mates at Adelaide to board the ship for England, he announced that he had never kept wickets in his life and had no intention of ever doing so!

As a result, Jack Blackham, who was one of the selectors responsible for the blunder, was forced to keep in nearly every match on the tour.

Doctor Runs

In the First Test at Lord's, Dr. John Barrett, who was making his Test debut, became the first batsman to carry his bat through a completed Test innings, when he made 67 out of Australia's second innings of 176. He played in only one more Test.

One Match or Many

Fred "Nutty" Martin, a left-arm bowler from Kent who was making his Test debut, spearheaded England's two-wicket win at The Oval in 1890 by taking 6/50 and 6/52. It remained his only Ashes appearance.

Syd Gregory, a diminutive stokemaker and brilliant cover fieldsman from NSW, who made his Test debut on the 1890 tour, went on to play in 52 Ashes Tests, a record that still stands. Allan Border (47) and Steve Waugh (46) have come closest to beating it, while Colin Cowdrey (43) holds the record for England.

Century Debuts

In the First Test at Lord's in 1893, Harry Graham (107) became the second Australian after Charlie Bannerman to make a hundred on his Test debut. It was his first hundred in first-class cricket and remarkably he also made his second first-class hundred in a Test match – at Sydney in February 1895.

The other Australians to make a hundred on Test debut in an Ashes Test are Reggie Duff (1901-02); Roger Hartigan (1907-08); Herbie Collins (1920-21); Bill Ponsford (1924-25); Archie Jackson (1928-29); Jim Burke (1950-51); Doug Walters (1965-66); Greg Chappell (1970-71); Dirk Welham (1981); Kepler Wessels (1982-83); Mark Waugh (1990-91); and Greg Blewett (1994-04). Graham and Welham are the only players to achieve it in England.

Dragging Defeat from Jaws of Victory

The opening Test of the 1894-95 series at Sydney provided the first of only three instances in Test history where a side has won after following-on. Batting first, Australia made the huge score of 586, which included innings of 201 by Syd Gregory and

Gilbert On the Run

England's win at The Oval was set up by a brilliant 104 from Gilbert Jessop, who reached his century in 75 minutes, still the fastest hundred in Ashes Tests. When last man in Wilfred Rhodes joined George Hirst, England still needed 15 runs to win, but the two Yorkshiremen calmly knocked off the runs with a minimum of fuss.

Record then Retire

England's five-wicket victory in the First Test at Sydney in 1903 was set up by R. E. Foster's 287, which is still the highest individual score by any player on his Test debut. It is also the highest Test score made by a visiting player in Australia, and stood as the highest score in all Test cricket until 1929-30. Due to business commitments, this was his only Test series against Australia.

Wet Rhodes

In the Second Test at Melbourne Wilfred Rhodes exploited a wet pitch to take 7/56 and 8/68. His match figures of 15/124 remained the best in an Ashes Test until Hedley Verity took 15/104 for England at Lord's in 1934.

Two Hats

Hugh Trumble became the only player to take two hat tricks in Ashes Tests when he performed the feat in England's second innings of the Fifth Test at Melbourne, his last Test (and first-class) match. His tally of 141 wickets stood as a record in Ashes Tests until 1981 when it was overtaken by Dennis Lillee. Lillee's subsequent record tally of 167 wickets in these matches was overhauled by Shane Warne in the final Test of the 2005 series.

69

Jack's Debut

The 1907-08 series marked the debut of Jack Hobbs, generally regarded as England's greatest-ever batsman. Hobbs' Test career lasted until 1930 and his tally of 3,636 runs at 54.26 in Ashes Tests is still the highest by an English batsman.

Almost a Tie

The Second Test at Melbourne in 1907-08 would have ended in the first tie in Test cricket, but with the scores level, England's last pair was able to scramble the winning run after cover point Gerry Hazlitt missed a straight-forward run out chance. In the previous Test at Sydney, Hazlitt, who was making his Test debut, was one of Australia's heroes, as he took part in an unbroken ninth wicket stand of 56 with "Tibby" Cotter to take Australia to a thrilling two-wicket win.

Still a Record

The eighth-wicket stand of 243 by Clem Hill (160) and debutant Roger Hartigan (116) in the Third Test at Adelaide in 1907-08 still stands as an Australian record in all Tests.

Leading with the Left

In the Fifth Test at The Oval in 1909, the New South Wales left-hander Warren Bardley, who was playing in his first Test series, made 136 and 130, making him the first batsman to score a hundred in each innings of a Test match. The only other Australians to perform the feat in Ashes Tests are ArthurMorris (1946-47); Steve Waugh (1997); and Matthew Hayden (2002-03). Englishmen to do so are Herbert Sutcliffe (1924-25); Wally Hammond (1928-29); and Denis Compton (1946-47).

Versatile Captain

C.B. Fry not only captained England in cricket, but played soccer for his nation and also equalled the world long-jump record.

Honourable Mention

England's captain in 1905, the Hon F. S. Jackson, not only led his country to a 2-0 series win, but won the toss in all five Tests and topped the series batting and bowling averages. He was born on the same day (21.11.1870) as his Australian counterpart, Joe Darling.

Worst Defeat

Australia suffered its worst defeat in an Ashes Test to date in 1911-12 when, after winning the First Test, it lost the next four to go down 4-1. Australia has suffered two more series defeats by a similar margin since – in 1928-29 and the infamous Bodyline series of 1932-33.

Board Blows and Strike

The escalating dispute between the Australian Cricket Board of Control, which had been formed in 1905, and the leading Australian players could not have helped the home side's performance. Matters came to a head at a selection meeting in Sydney prior to the Fourth Test, when Clem Hill, the Australian captain, and former Test player Peter McAlister, a board man, came to blows after McAlister accused Hill of being the worst captain he had ever seen.

The brawl lasted for 20 minutes and made newspaper headlines the next day, McAlister emerging from the altercation with cuts to his nose and face and a black eye. Not

surprisingly England won the Adelaide Test by an innings and 225 runs, after Jack Hobbs (178) and Wilfred Rhodes (179) put on 323 for the first wicket, which is still England's record opening partnership in Ashes Tests. Rhodes' rise up the batting order was remarkable as he had begun his Test career in 1899 as a No. 11 batsman.

Tour Disaster

The aftermath of the dispute between the players and the Board was that six leading Australian players – Clem Hill, Victor Trumper, Warwick Armstrong, Vernon Ransford, Hanson Carter and "Tibby" Cotter – dubbed the "Big Six" by the press – refused to tour England in 1912. This was over the Board's refusal to appoint Frank Laver, who had been a popular and capable player/manager on the 1905 and 1909 tours, as manager for the 1912 tour.

The depleted 1912 Australians did poorly in England losing the three Test Ashes Series 1-0. This was the year of the ill-fated Triangular Tournament which saw South Africa also tour England, with the three countries playing three Tests against each other. A combination of poor weather, the weak Australian side and a poor showing by the South Africans, meant that the experiment was a disaster.

Australia Whitewash

The first Test series after the First World War, in 1920-21, produced the only "whitewash" in Ashes history, with Australia trouncing England 5-0. The only other time a side has won five Tests in an Ashes Series was in 1978-79, when Mike Brearley's defeated an Australian side weakened by defections to World Series Cricket, 5-1.

The Big Ship

The 1920-21 series was a triumph for Australia's new skipper, the 41-year-old Warwick Armstrong, who at around 20 stone is almost certainly the heaviest man to appear in Ashes Tests. He led from the front, making three hundreds and taking valuable wickets with his leg breaks.

Arthur and Jack

Two newcomers starred for Australia. Leg break and googly bowler Arthur Mailey took 36 wickets in the series despite not bowling a ball in the Second Test, a tally that remained an Ashes record for Australia until Rodney Hogg took 41 wickets in 1978-79. His figures of 9/121 in the Fourth Test at Melbourne are still the best for Australia in all Tests. Another star was the dynamic all-rounder Jack Gregory who scored 442 runs, took 23 wickets and held 15 catches.

One Ball Career

By contrast the popular Roy Park, who had been scoring heavily for Victoria, was bowled first ball in the Second Test in Melbourne and never received another chance at Test level. His wife was watching the game while she knitted. She dropped her needles as he came into bat and looked down to pick them up. As a result she missed seeing his entire Test career. Their son-in-law Ian Johnson went onto captain Australia.

Test Caps Going Cheap

Australia extended its winning sequence to eight, when it won the first three Tests of the 1921 series in England. The home team was so demoralised that its selectors called upon 30 players in the series, of whom 17 appeared only once.

73

Debut at 33

In 1925 in the final Test at Sydney, 33-year-old New Zealand-born leg spinner Clarrie Grimmett took 5/45 and 6/37 on his Test debut. Despite his late start, Grimmett went to take 106 wickets in Ashes Tests, and became the first player from any country to take 200 Test wickets.

Recall at 48

Australia's winning run came to an end in 1926 when set 415 to win, Australia managed only 125 when Wilfred Rhodes, who was recalled after a five-year absence to play his final Ashes Test at the age of 48, captured 4/44.

Never too old

Earlier in the 1926 series 40-year-old Charlie Macartney, made three hundreds in a row for Australia. At Lord's in the Second Test, the 43-year-old Warren Bardsley, who like Macartney was playing in his last Test series, carried his bat for 193 in Australia's first innings of 383.

Archie Jackson. What if?

Don Bradman made his debut in the 1928-29 series and finished with 468 runs at 66.85, but Australia's batting averages were headed by the gifted 19-year-old Archie Jackson, who made a superb 164 at Adelaide on his Test debut. Sadly, Jackson was to die from tuberculosis just four years later.

Wally Found

Bradman and Jackson were overshadowed, however, by another Ashes debutant, England's Wally Hammond. Hammond became the first player to score consecutive Test double hundreds when he made 251 at Sydney in the Second

Right: Steve Waugh after hitting the winning runs in the Second Test at Lord's. Boon 58 not out.
Graham Morris Photography

Husband in the Dressing Room *by Pip Boon*

We started going out when were teenagers and have been together ever since. He was at Launceston Grammar and I was at the girls' school, Oakburn College.

I thought he was special and very funny. But cricket!

I came from a family of girls and knew nothing about the game, but luckily our home was within walking distance to the ground where David played. I could go down and watch for a while and then head home to finish my homework.

Looking back I seemed to spend an incredible amount of time waiting for him outside dressing rooms.

And of course during David's playing years wives were never made to feel overly welcome.

I can remember when David was captain of an Australian 'A' team playing in Hobart and I was not allowed into the facilities to breast feed our baby.

I had to resort to the hill where it was bitterly cold but thankfully a journalist in the press box saw me and invited me in there to finish feeding. Needless to say I didn't stay at that match for long.

That was typical of the time.

Some of the tours lasted for four months and if any wives had the audacity to join their husbands, they were only welcome for the last week or so.

The players stayed at plush hotels and we stayed at cheap bread-and-breakfasts. We were not allowed to step a foot inside the players' hotel. But if you were a single guy of course you could have a girl friend come and visit!

It certainly wasn't glamorous or easy being a cricketer's wife. In fact many players spent their tour fee paying to bring their wives on tour – even if they were staying at the cheap hotel down the road.

But there were good times which we enjoyed together and the depths which we endured together. A number of times I would get a late night call from David at home in Launceston after a bad day with the bat and be on the first plane the next morning to a Test match somewhere in Australia after dropping our kids off at my mothers.

The time spent apart was reflected in the phone bill.

The worst time was undoubtedly when he was dropped. We had a motto that said "you had to hit rock bottom before you could climb up again." We certainly did.

But he was always very focused.

Pip, shedding a tear at my last game.

Hutton's Record

England found a batsman to match Bradman's dominance with the emergence of 22-year-old Yorkshireman Len Hutton. Australia retained the Ashes but England managed to square the series with the biggest win in Test history. Hutton scored 364 in a marathon 797 minutes. It broke Bradman's Test record set eight years earlier and the Don was the first to shake his hand when he passed his score.

Bradman subsequently broke an ankle when he stepped in a hole while bowling and took no further part in the match. England scored 7-903 declared and won by an innings and 579 runs, the biggest margin in history.

Should have Chucked

'Chuck' Fleetwood-Smith, the Australian left-arm wrist spinner, finished with 1/298 from 87 overs. To compound matters for Australia, Bradman and Fingleton were both injured and were unable to bat in either innings.

Hostilities Resume

After the Second World War in 1946, Australia won the First Test at the Gabba by an innings and 332 runs. Don Bradman, whose return to Test cricket had been in great doubt following a period of ill health, made 187. He began uncertainly and at 28 was controversially adjudged not out when he appeared to slice a catch to second slip. From that point on his confidence returned and he went on to head Australia's batting averages with 680 runs at 97.14.

Welcome

Keith Miller, Ray Lindwall and Arthur Morris all made their Ashes debuts in this series. Miller took 7/60 in the First Test and

made an unbeaten 141 in the Fourth Test at Adelaide, Lindwall ended the series by taking 7/63 at Sydney and hit a whirlwind 100 in the Third Test at Melbourne, while Morris scored a hundred in each innings of the Fourth Test at Adelaide.

Invincibles

Dubbed the "Invincibles", the Australian side that toured England in 1948 is regarded as the strongest of all time, and went through the entire tour without losing a match. Led by Don Bradman in his farewell series, it trounced England 4-0. A highlight was Australia's win in the Fourth Test at Leeds when, set 404 to win on a turning pitch in under a day, it reached its target for the loss of only three wickets following a partnership of 301 by Arthur Morris (182) and Bradman (173 not out).

In Australia's first innings, the 19-year-old Neil Harvey made 112 on his Ashes debut and Sam Loxton, in his second Ashes Test, hit five sixes in a whirlwind 93. In the Fifth Test at The Oval, Ray Lindwall took 6/20 to rout England for 52 in its first innings, its lowest Ashes score on home soil.

They're a Weird Mob

In 1950-51 the bowling averages were headed by 35-year-old mystery spinner Jack Iverson, whose extraordinary folded finger grip enabled him to obtain exceptional spin and bounce combined with remarkable accuracy. His virtually undetectable leg breaks, wrong' uns and top-spinners netted him 21 wickets at 15.23, with best figures of 6/27 at Sydney, in what turned out to be his only Test series. Amazingly he had played virtually no cricket until he was 31.

Typhoon Damage

Australia looked likely to regain the Ashes 1954-55 after

big hundreds by Arthur Morris and Neil Harvey enabled it to win the First Test at the Gabba by an innings and 154 runs. Then, in a remarkable reversal of form, England won the next three Tests. This was largely due to the explosive fast bowling of Ashes newcomer, Frank 'Typhoon' Tyson, who took 4/45 and 6/85 in the Second Test at Sydney followed by a devastating 7/27 in Australia's second innings in the next Test at Melbourne.

Tyson was well supported at the other end by the perennially accurate Brian Statham, while Peter May and another Ashes newcomer, Colin Cowdrey, who was making the first of his six tours of Australia, batted impressively. Tyson later settled in Australia teaching at Carey Grammar in Melbourne, where he coached former Test captain Graham Yallop, and commentated on radio and television.

Spinning in a Winner

Having lost the last three Ashes Series, Australia, under the inspiring captaincy of the newly-appointed Richie Benaud, convincingly won the 1958-59 series 4-0 against an England side widely believed to be one the strongest ever sent to Australia.

Benaud's leg breaks netted 31 wickets at 18.83, while Colin McDonald (520 runs at 65.00) was the leading batsman in a generally low-scoring series. The left-arm fast bowling of Alan Davidson and Ian Meckiff also played a big role in Australia's success. Neil Harvey's 167 at Melbourne in the Second Test was the first hundred for Australia in an Ashes Test since the opening match of the 1954-55 series.

A remarkable spell from Benaud, who bowled around the wicket and pitched his leg breaks into the bowlers' footmarks took Australia to an unexpected 54-run victory in the Fourth Test at Manchester in 1961. Set 256 to win, England lost its last nine wickets for 51 runs, as Benaud took 5/12 in 25 balls to

finish with 6/70. In the previous Test, at Leeds, Fred Trueman bowled England to victory with match figures of 11 for 88, including a spell of 5/0 in the second innings.

Non-Core Promises

Following the memorable cricket in the Australia versus West Indies series of 1960-61, the opposing Ashes captains in 1962-63, Richie Benaud and Ted Dexter, promised to play entertaining cricket. However, with the series level at one-all after the Third Test, the last two Tests ended in dull draws, making it the first five-Test series in Australia to end in a stalemate.

Dull, Dull, Dull, Dull

Bob Simpson led the 1964 Australian team to England on which four of the five Tests were drawn. The only Test to produce a result was the Third, at Leeds, where a magnificent 160 from Peter Burge enabled Australia to recover from a precarious 7/178 to make 389 and go on to win by seven wickets.

Needing only to draw the following Test, at Manchester, to make sure of retaining the Ashes, Simpson occupied the crease throughout the first two days, batting in all for 12 hours and 42 minutes to make 311, his first Test hundred and the second highest score by an Australian in Ashes Tests.

Australia declared at eight for 656 on the third morning. With a message to prove England batted for almost the remainder of the match to make 611, with Ken Barrington making 256 and Ted Dexter 174. Tom Veivers (3/155) bowled 95.1 overs, the most in a single innings in an Ashes Test.

Ashes Back To England

After the longest series in Test history, England regained the Ashes in 1970-71 after an absence of 12 years. With the

WACA Ground in Perth staging its initial Test, the Ashes were fought over six Tests for the first time. Then, after no play was possible on the first three days of the Third Test at Melbourne, the authorities abandoned the match and scheduled an additional Test in Melbourne in its place, a move that netted the Australian Board an additional $135,000 in gate money. On the scheduled last day of the abandoned Test, Australia defeated England by five wickets in a hastily-scheduled one-day match that is now regarded as the first One-Day International.

Phanto at the Crease then Gone

In the Fourth Test only skipper Bill Lawry, who carried his bat for 60 in Australia's second innings of 116, could withstand fast bowler John Snow, who finished with 7/40. Lawry became only the fifth Australian to bat through a completed innings in Ashes Tests, after Jack Barrett, Warren Bardsley, Bill Woodfull (twice), and Bill Brown. With Australia 1-0 down coming in to the final Test, Lawry was sensationally dropped and replaced as captain by Ian Chappell.

In a tense and bitter match, England clinched the Ashes when it won by 62 runs. Crowd disturbances late on the second day, after Snow had hit Australian tail-ender Terry Jenner on the head with a short-pitched ball, saw England captain Ray Illingworth lead his side off the field without consulting the umpires.

Play resumed after the umpires warned him that the match would be awarded to Australia if he did not return.

Chappelli Skipper

The appointment of Ian Chappell as captain laid the foundation for the aggressive approach that has characterised the modern Australian approach. Although it failed to regain

the Ashes in England in 1972, Australia acquitted itself well, levelling the series two-all.

Dennis Lillee, who took 31 wickets, emerged as an outstanding fast bowler, while Keith Stackpole (485 runs) and Greg Chappell (437) scored heavily. After losing the First Test, Australia levelled the series in the Second Test at Lord's, thanks to an amazing exhibition of swing bowling by Bob Massie who took 8/84 and 8/53 on his Test debut to achieve the best match analysis by an Australian bowler in all Tests. I watched this on TV in Launceston. It was as if he was bowling boomerangs!

After the Third Test was drawn, England won the Fourth Test at Leeds by nine wickets to retain the Ashes, after Australia collapsed twice on a sub-standard pitch that greatly assisted the home side. Australia squared the rubber when it won the Fifth Test at The Oval by five wickets, after an enthralling contest in which Ian (118) and Greg Chappell (113) became the first brothers to score hundreds in the same Test innings.

Lillian Thomson

Australia regained the Ashes in devastating fashion in 1974-75, winning the rubber 4-1 in a series dominated by the fearsome fast bowling duo of Dennis Lillee and Jeff Thomson. Lillee, who had missed the previous season with a serious back injury, took 25 wickets, while Thomson, virtually unknown before the series, took 33 wickets at 17.93 before missing the final Test after injuring himself playing tennis.

Dougie!

Australia's nine-wicket victory in the Second Test at Perth was highlighted by a brilliant century by Doug Walters. He was my idol as I grew up and I worshipped him. In the first hour after tea on the second day he made 67, and he pulled the last

ball of the day, from Bob Willis, over the square leg fence for six to bring up his century and 100 runs in the session. Way to go!

Centenary of Ashes

To celebrate the 100th anniversary of the inaugural Test match, played at Melbourne in March 1877, a Centenary Test match was staged at the MCG on March 12-17, 1977.

All living former players and umpires from previous Ashes encounters, as well as leading officials, were invited to Melbourne to watch the match and attend special events organised by the Australian Cricket Board, the Victorian Cricket Association and the Melbourne Cricket Club. Amazingly the result – victory to Australia by 45 runs – was identical to that in the very first Test.

Australia's stars were Dennis Lillee, who took 6/26 and 5/139, and Rod Marsh, whose 110 not out in the second innings was the first hundred by an Australian keeper in an Ashes Test. In Australia's second innings, David Hookes, who was making his Test debut, hit England's skipper Tony Greig for five consecutive fours. In England's second innings, Derek Randall, on his Ashes debut, hit a memorable 174 to win the Man of the Match award.

World Series Leads to Woeful Performance

Soon after the 1977 Australian team arrived in England came the shock announcement that 13 of its 17 members had secretly signed contracts to play World Series Cricket over the following two Australian summers. As a result Australia suffered its heaviest loss in England since the 1880s, losing the series 3-0.

Mike Brearley captained England for the first time and proved a highly astute leader, while Bob Willis obtained three

five-wicket hauls to capture 27 wickets in the series and Geoff Boycott returned from a self-imposed four-year exile to make 107 and 80 not out at in the Third Test at Nottingham and 191 at Leeds in the following Test.

Ian Botham made an impressive start to his Test career by taking 5/74 in Australia's first innings at Nottingham.

From Woeful to Worst

Weakened by the absence of its World Series players, Australia was no match for England in 1978-79, losing the series 5-1 to suffer its worst-ever Ashes defeat.

The only bright spot for Australia was the fast bowling of my old mate Rodney Hogg, who began his Test career with 6/74 in the First Test at Brisbane and followed up with 5/65 and 5/57 at Perth in the Second Test and 5/30 and 5/36 in the Third Test at Melbourne, the only match Australia won. By the end of the series he had taken 41 wickets at 12.85. It is still the record tally for an Ashes Series in Australia. If you don't believe me then ask him. He still answers to 41@12.85.

Not the Real Thing

Following the peace settlement between the Australian Cricket Board and the World Series organisation, a three-Test series between Australia and England was staged in 1979-80. With its leading players back, Australia was much stronger and won all three matches. However England retained the Ashes, as the English authorities decided that because it was only a three-match series the Ashes were not at stake.

In the First Test at Perth, Dennis Lillee faced four balls using an aluminium bat. After scoring three runs, the England captain, Mike Brearley demanded that he stop using it. An argument ensued and play was held up for 10 minutes before he

Right: Boony passing on the song at his last game.

reverted to a wooden bat.

As always Rodney Hogg was in the thick of it. As 12th man for Australia he was the "bat carrier" and had an eye witness account of it. The language from Lillee was only surpassed by skipper Greg Chappell and even Hoggie copped a spray from both players as he carried bats on and off the field.

Subsequently the Laws of Cricket were amended to state that the bat must be made of wood.

Poor Imitation

Following the success of the Centenary Test at Melbourne in 1977, England staged a Centenary Test at Lord's on August 28-September 2, 1980 to commemorate the anniversary of the first Test in England, which was played at The Oval in September 1880.

Although the events associated with the match were a big success, the Test itself, for which the Ashes were again not at stake, was a huge disappointment and ended in a dull draw. The only bright spot was the superb batting of Kim Hughes, who scored 117 and 84 for Australia. Rain delays badly affected the match and some Marylebone Cricket Club members became so infuriated by the seemingly unnecessary delays that they scuffled with one of the umpires as he returned to the pavilion after one of the many pitch inspections on the third day.

Botham Nightmare

The Third Test at Leeds was the most extraordinary contest in Ashes history. England recalled Mike Brearley to replace the out-of-form Ian Botham as captain. But the move appeared to have back-fired when Australia gained a first innings lead of 227 and, after enforcing the follow-on, had England reeling at 7/135 in its second innings. Still needing 92 to avoid an innings defeat,

and with only three wickets in hand, Australia appeared certain to go 2-0 up in the series.

So hopeless did England's position appear that bookmakers Ladbrokes, from their tent on the ground, were offering odds of 500 to 1 for an England victory.

Freed from the cares of captaincy and revelling in the nothing-to-lose situation, Ian Botham then launched an amazing assault on the Australian bowlers, especially Dennis Lillee and Terry Alderman. In the last session of the fourth day, England added 175 runs in 27 overs, and at the close of the day had built up a lead of 124, which it extended to 130 before the innings closed early next day. Botham was 149 run out, having received grand support from tail-enders Graham Dilley and Chris Old.

Facing a modest target, Australia still appeared certain to win, but Bob Willis, in an inspired spell of fast bowling, took a career-best 8/43, which saw Australia collapse from 1/56 to 111 all out. England's 18-run victory stretched the bounds of belief and provided only the second instance in Test history of a side winning after following-on. It left the Aussies shell shocked.

Bet On It

The result had a bizarre sequel 18 months later, when Dennis Lillee revealed in his autobiography that, as a joke, he and Rod Marsh had laid a bet of £15 with Ladbrokes on an England victory at the 500/1 odds offered on the fourth day of the Test. Following England's unbelievable victory they collected £7500 ($A15,000).

The Australian Cricket Board was none too pleased when it found out, and although it took no action against Lillee and Marsh, it inserted a clause banning players in future from betting

on matches in which they took part.

... and again

History repeated itself in the very next Test, at Birmingham, as Australia again lost another apparently unloseable match. Having led by 69 on the first innings, it dismissed England for a modest 219 in its second innings, and needed just 151 to win.

When it moved past 100 still with six wickets in hand, victory seemed assured, but Ian Botham produced another epic performance as he captured five wickets for one run in 28 balls. Australia's last six wickets crashed for just 16 to give England a 29-run victory. No batsman in the match reached 50, with Mike Brearley's 48 on the opening day remaining the highest score.

... and again, again

The demoralised Australians lost the next Test at Manchester, where Ian Botham hit a record six sixes in a whirlwind 118 in England's second innings, before drawing the final Test at The Oval. Remarkably, despite losing the rubber 3-1, the leading batsman and bowlers in the series were Australians.

Allan Border was by far the leading run-scorer with 533 at 59.22, while Terry Alderman (42 at 21.26) and Dennis Lillee (39 at 22.30) were the leading wicket-takers. Alderman's tally is still the record for an Australian bowler in an Ashes Series.

Only in Australia

Australia won the 1982-83 series 2-1, thereby regaining the Ashes which it had lost in England in 1977. The opening Test at Perth, which ended in a draw, was marred by an ugly crowd invasion by drunken spectators on the second day.

During the invasion, Terry Alderman was punched from behind, and in tackling his assailant to the ground,

he dislocated his shoulder so badly that he was unable to play again during the season. He returned to be a match winner and it was an honour to play beside him, but his repertoire of deliveries, especially his in-swinging cutter, was limited. How great could he have been?

South African Aussie

In the Second Test, Kepler Wessels became the first South African-born player to represent Australia, and marked his debut by making 162 and 46, while Geoff Lawson took 11 wickets. Needing 292 to win, Australia appeared to be in a hopeless position when its ninth wicket fell at 218. But with Allan Border shielding Jeff Thomson from the strike, the last pair took the score to 255 by stumps on the fourth day and on the last morning, 18,000 spectators, admitted free of charge, watched in great excitement as the pair edged Australia towards an Ashes-clinching victory.

Then, with four runs needed for victory, Thomson edged Botham's first delivery of the eighteenth over of the day to Chris Tavaré at second slip. Although he dropped the ball, Geoff Miller at first slip caught it on the rebound to give England a three-run victory – a result that equalled the closest in Ashes Tests to that time, by Australia at Manchester in 1902. A draw in the final Test at Sydney ensured that Australia regained the Ashes.

Tasmanian Heritage

I began my Ashes career in the 1985 series, but apart from top-scoring with 61 in Australia's first innings in the Fourth Test at Manchester, struggled with the conditions. I was only the third Tasmanian representative to appear in an Ashes Test, following Kenny Burn (1890) and Charles Eady (1896 and

1901-02), although Jack Badcock and Max Walker both played Test cricket after moving to the mainland.

Laurie Nash was playing for Tasmania at the time of his Test debut against South Africa in 1931-32, but had returned to his native Victoria by the time of his only Ashes Test in 1936-37.

Losers Please Themselves

In 1987 Australia salvaged some pride by winning the final Test at Sydney by 55 runs, ending a sequence of 14 Tests against all countries without a win. Australia's stars were Dean Jones, who made an unbeaten 184 in the first innings and off-spinner Peter Taylor, who took 6/78 in England's first innings and made an important 42 when Australia batted a second time. Taylor, dubbed "Peter Who?" by the press, was a shock selection, for he had played only once for his State during the season and only six first-class matches in all. As the Australian side contained only one specialist opening batsman, following my omission, many felt that the selectors had meant to include his namesake in the New South Wales team, Mark Taylor.

Boon's Bicentenary

A one-off Bicentenary Test was played at Sydney in 1988, to commemorate 200 years of white settlement in Australia. Australia was made to follow-on on 211 runs in arrears, but easily saved the game, making 2/328 in its second innings. My future was at the cross roads but in this innings I shared an opening stand of 162 with Geoff Marsh, and batted for over eight hours to make an unbeaten 184. The innings relaunched my career.

Winning and Grinning Again

The 1989 Ashes tour of England marked the start of a golden era for Australian cricket. It entered the series having won just nine out of the 38 Ashes Tests played since the Centenary Test at Melbourne in March 1977, and had won only one series during that time. By contrast, from 1989 to 2002-03 Australia won a record eight Ashes Series in a row, winning 28 Tests to England's seven.

Lanky Leftie

In 1990-91 in the Second Test Bruce Reid was Australia's outstanding bowler, taking 6/97 and 7/51. In the second innings he and Greg Matthews brought about an extraordinary batting collapse which saw England lose its last six wickets for three runs in 12 overs.

Two draws, followed by a nine-wicket victory at Perth in the final Test ensured that Australia retained the Ashes. I hit my straps on the quicker strips and was the leading run-scorer in the series, making 530 runs at 75.71, while Reid with 27 wickets at 16.00 in four Tests was the leading bowler.

Vintage Series

Australia convincingly retained the Ashes in 1993, winning the six-match rubber 4-1. It began by winning the opening Test at Manchester by 191 runs, a match made memorable by Shane Warne's first Ashes delivery, a vicious leg break which pitched outside the leg stump and hit the top of Mike Gatting's off stump. Warne finished with eight wickets in the match and took 34 in the series, launching a career which saw him become the leading wicket-taker in Ashes Tests.

In the Second Test at Lord's, Mark Taylor (111) and Michael Slater (152 in his second Test match) put on 260 for

95

the first wicket, before I managed an unbeaten 164 which took Australia to 4/632 declared and an eventual innings victory.

Australia exceeded this total in the Fourth Test at Leeds where I was lucky enough to make my third hundred in successive Tests, before a huge unbroken fifth wicket stand of 332 by Allan Border (200 not out) and Steve Waugh (157 not out) took Australia to 4/653 declared.

I managed to be the leading run-scorer for the second Ashes Series in a row with 555 runs at 69.37. Warne's 34 wickets cost 25.79 apiece and he was well supported by Merv Hughes, who took 31 wickets in his last Ashes Series. This was also Allan Border's last series against England – his 433 runs at 54.12 took his overall tally in these matches to 3,548 runs at 56.31, the third-highest aggregate on record.

Vintage Warne

Two emphatic wins in the first two Tests set up Australia's 3-1 win in the 1994-95 Ashes rubber. In the opening Test at Brisbane, Shane Warne recorded his best Test figures of 8/71 in England's second innings.

The Second Test at Melbourne, which Australia won by 295 runs, was ended by a hat trick by Warne, the first in an Ashes Test since Hugh Trumble's on the same ground 91 years earlier. Warne's victims were Phil DeFreitas, Darren Gough and Devon Malcolm, the last to a diving catch at short leg by yours truly. On that day you could hear the ball "fizz" through the air after leaving his hand. It was eerie. England, set 388 to win, was all out for 92. Earlier I had managed a very dour 131 on a difficult, two-paced pitch. To this day I think it was one of my finest efforts because the pitch was a shocker.

Allan Border looks back at his "Loyal Lieutenant" and fellow Australian selector

The infamous tied Test in Madras was undoubtedly one of David Boon's finest moments. He made a remarkable century in the stifling conditions, which almost killed Dean Jones.

Then in the field as my vice captain and able lieutenant he was outstanding.

Late on the last day the match was in the balance, the temperature was rising, the conditions were deplorable. It was tight and tense. Every ball was a story in itself. Field placements were important – vital in fact.

So I was taking my time setting my field. Suddenly one of the Indian umpires chastised me for wasting time!

I took a mighty verbal crack at the umpire and told him what I thought of his abilities and that I would move my field about as and when I liked.

He then threatened to send me off!

I looked around for support and saw my highly esteemed and very knowledgeable vice captain.

"Boony, he cannot send me off! Can he?" I asked.

"F****d if I know. You're the captain," he said and waddled off.

With that sort of support I immediately apologised to the umpire and back-peddled my way out of trouble.

In South Africa, after a big win, we had been celebrating into the early hours and then back to the hotel for some sleep before packing to catch a pre-dawn flight.

Always keen to be one step ahead of the pack the little keg on legs decided to pack his bags, take them down to reception and just leave his travelling clothes and small carry bag beside his bed for the morning. Just the bare essentials.

That way he could steal an extra hour in bed.

Smart move and good thinking.

He duly packed everything away and then towed his bags down the corridor to the lift and down to the foyer where our cricket gear was already being stored.

As he came out of the lift one of the South African porters saw him and exclaimed excitedly: "Mr Boon, Mr Boon, let me take your bags."

"No, I will be right mate," was the response.

"No Mr Boon, I insist. I will take your bags," said a most persistent porter as he began walking in front of the vice captain of Australia.

Boony was becoming irate.

"I'm okay. I am quite capable of taking my bags over there."

"No Mr Boon, please. You must listen to me. You are wearing no clothes!"

Boon has often been a pain in the arse but personally he was at his worst in New Zealand in a tour in the early 90s.

Near the end of the trip we were in the bus for yet another long dash to yet another match and the boys became restive. Then they decided a bit of wrestling would pass the time.

As captain I tried to remain aloof from these shenanigans as the aisle quickly filled with the cream of Australian cricket hurling themselves at each other.

Then a very young Damien Martyn came over the back seat and tried a few of his favourite holds on me.

He quickly had me on the floor when suddenly I felt this dreadful pain in my backside.

I quickly looked over my shoulder and there was David Boon with his teeth in my arse! And he wouldn't let go. I tried pushing him off but I had Bulldog Boon biting my bum.

He finally relented but two days later I had to face my suspicious wife with this mysterious fang mark on my backside.

But after a careful wifely examination – like something from the TV series CSI – I was exonerated!

The bite mark had a part missing in the middle, which exactly matched the gap in the front of the Boon teeth.

Allan Border after the Second Test against England in 1990. Geoff Marsh and I had batted out the day to win. *Gregg Porteous Photography*

Winning Streak

Australia achieved a record fifth-successive Ashes Series win in 1997 despite losing the First Test at Birmingham by nine wickets. England managed to draw the second, at Lord's, despite being dismissed for 77 in its first innings, when Glenn McGrath took 8/38. But England was heavily defeated in each of the next three.

The stars for Australia in the Fourth Test were three players appearing in their first Ashes series: Matthew Elliott, who scored 199 and Ricky Ponting 127 and Jason Gillespie, who took 7/37 in England's first innings.

In the second innings, Paul Reiffel, who had been summoned from Australia to reinforce the team, took 5/49.

Elliott with 556 runs at 55.60 was easily Australia's most successful batsman, while Glenn McGrath's 36 wickets cost only 19.47 apiece.

Long

In 1997-98 the Fourth Test in Melbourne was a remarkable contest, which England won by 12 runs after Australia was set a modest target of 175 to win. After the first day's play was washed out, extra time was added to the remaining days, and the last day, which lasted 483 minutes, was the longest in Test history.

Dean Headley, whose grandfather, the legendary George, and father Ron, had both played for the West Indies, was England's most successful bowler, taking 6/60 in Australia's second innings.

Spinning Stuart

The final Test at Sydney was an eventful match, which Australia won by 98 runs. After Mark Taylor, who was playing in his final Test, won the toss for the fifth time in the

series, and the 11th time in his last 12 Ashes Tests, Australia slumped from 5/319 to 322 all out. Darren Gough dismissed Ian Healy, Stuart MacGill and Colin Miller with successive deliveries to complete the first hat trick by an Englishman in an Ashes Test since J.T. Hearne at Leeds in 1899.

Australia's bowling star was Stuart MacGill who finished with match figures of 12/107. By contrast, Shane Warne, in his only appearance of the series, managed just 2/110.

Welcome Gilly

Australia commenced its defence of the Ashes in 2001 in emphatic fashion with a crushing win by an innings and 118 runs in the opening Test at Birmingham. Adam Gilchrist smashed 152 off 143 balls. Gilchrist, playing in his first Test against England, and Glenn McGrath put on 63 for the last wicket, towards which McGrath contributed just a single.

Batsmen bow to Bowlers

Despite the success of its batsmen in the series, Australia's stars were Glenn McGrath and Shane Warne, who captured 63 wickets between them, including seven five-wicket hauls.

Keep on Rolling

Australia's eighth consecutive win of an Ashes Series in 2002-03 was perhaps the most convincing of the lot, for it won each of the first four Tests by a wide margin, before England salvaged some pride by winning the final Test at Sydney. England got off to a bad start in the opening Test at Brisbane, where Nasser Hussain sent Australia in to bat after winning the toss, only for Australia to end the first day at 2/364, following centuries by Matthew Hayden and Ricky Ponting.

Hayden hit another hundred in the second innings, before Glenn McGrath and Shane Warne routed England for 79 in its second innings to give Australia victory by 384 runs. The result of the series was decided by Christmas, as Australia won by an innings at 51 runs at Adelaide and by an innings and 48 runs at Perth to go 3-0 up.

Farewell Steve

Australia went into the final Test without Glenn McGrath and Shane Warne, who were both injured. Only one run separated the sides on the first innings, but a superb 183 by Michael Vaughan in the second innings gave England the ascendancy and it went on to win by 225 runs. Steve Waugh ended his Ashes career with a dashing century in Australia's first innings, reaching his hundred from the last ball of the second day amid delirious scenes from his home crowd. It was his tenth Ashes hundred, a tally exceeded only by Don Bradman (19) and Jack Hobbs (12) and assisted his final tally in 46 Ashes Tests to 3,200 runs at 58.18.

England Borrow the Ashes

Australia's record-breaking run finally came to an end in 2005.

First Test – With Glenn McGrath taking nine wickets, Australia opened its defence of the Ashes with a convincing win by 239 runs in the first Test at Lord's but that proved to be its only win of the rubber.

Second Test – England promptly levelled the series with an extraordinary two-run victory, the closest in Ashes history, in the Second Test at Birmingham. After England piled on 407 on the opening day, with Brett Lee conceding 111 runs from 17 overs, Australia was eventually set 282 to win. At 7/137 and

later 8/175, an Australian victory seemed out of the question, but its tail-enders would not give in, until amid unbearable tension, a lifting delivery from Steve Harmison struck Michael Kasprowicz on the left glove and keeper Geraint Jones took a diving catch. Lee and Kasprowicz had added 59 for the tenth wicket in a remarkable, but ultimately fruitless partnership.

Third Test – There was further excitement in the Third Test at Manchester where, after skipper Michael Vaughan contributed 166 to England's first innings of 444, an outstanding rearguard century from his opposite number Ricky Ponting enabled Australia to salvage a draw after its last pair, Lee and McGrath saw out the last four overs.

Fourth Test – England had gained the ascendancy by now, however, and it won the Fourth Test at Nottingham by three wickets after Australia had been made to follow-on 259 in arrears.

Fifth Test – Now 2-1 down in the series, the visitors needed to win the last Test at The Oval to square the series, but never appeared likely to do so, as rain delays ensured that it ended in a draw, much to the jubilation of England supporters, overjoyed at seeing their side regain the Ashes after an interval of 16 years.

Records

Shane Warne took 6/122 and 6/124 in the match to lift his tally in the series to 40, taking his total in Ashes Tests to 172 at 22.30, five more than the previous record-holder Dennis Lillee. In England's second innings Kevin Pietersen hit seven sixes in his innings of 158, the most in an Ashes Test. In an even team performance, England's undoubted star was Andrew Flintoff who made 402 runs and took 24 wickets, while newcomer Pietersen (473) was the leading run-scorer.

CAPTAINS COURAGEOUS

Kim Hughes

My first Test match for Australia was Kim Hughes' last! He resigned with tears in his eyes just prior to another drubbing from the West Indies knowing he was leading a team that appeared to me, to be split in factions.

Of course I knew nothing of that at the time I was just a debutant breathing in the atmosphere of Test cricket. After three centuries in four innings in State cricket I was hopeful of a call up to the Test team but at the same time thinking I was undoubtedly unworthy of the honour. I was in the far west of Victoria at Portland playing in a commemorative game against the Victorians when I received a message at the lunch break to call the Australian team manager, Bob Merriman. He bluntly told me to get to Brisbane. From there it's all a bit of a haze.

I rang my wife and then my parents and that evening travelled in the team bus to Tullamarine and, while they headed for the Hobart flight, I was looking around for the lounge for the Brisbane flight. A few hours later I walked into my room and there laid out on the bed was my Australian uniform.

Cap, blazer, jumper, tracksuit, training gear. It was all there in front of me. It was a surreal experience and I just stood there breathing in the moment.

The next morning I was in the Australian dressing room seeking a quiet corner where no one would notice me. I headed for the traditional spot near the shower, which is always for the new boy and plonked myself down – right next to Allan Border. I had only met him once or twice before but it was the start of a long and ongoing friendship.

His first piece of advice to me was simple and subtle. It is forever etched in my memory.

"If you are about to say anything in here, make sure you are 200% right!" I didn't open my mouth for weeks as a result. In fact I was overawed.

My magical moment came in that match when I caught the great Viv Richards off Geoff Lawson at square leg. I was elated and the congratulations came thick and fast from my team mates.

It had been a single handed snatch low to the ground and my new team mates were quick to quip, "One hand, one bounce. That's a great way to start your career against the West Indies."

They kept implying the catch was taken on the bounce. By the end of the day I was beginning to believe them. Back in the dressing room I made some feeble excuse about going

out for a second and sneaked around to the Channel 9 van and asked them to replay the catch. Sure enough, it was a clean take. Much relieved I sneaked back into the rooms again. I didn't say a word but from then on, I always took advice about fielding with a grain of salt.

Another incident proved that you don't need enemies when you've got friends like West Indian speedster, Michael Holding. "Whispering Death", as he was known because of his frighteningly quiet approach to the wicket, had played in Tasmania and on hearing of my selection, rung my father to pass on his congratulations – but asked for it not to be made public.

That was fine off the field but on the field he very nearly turned me into a eunuch. He was bowling frighteningly fast on the quick Gabba wicket and reared a number of deliveries up near my groin. I fended them off but then the big fellow got one to crash through my defences and directly into the family jewels. I have never felt so much pain in my life and thought, if this is Test cricket then it's not everything it's cracked up to be.

The blow shook me and I only made a handful of runs. So in the second innings I was determined to try and get even with the West Indians. Late in the innings tail-ender Rodney Hogg came to the wicket and immediately said: "Babs, this is the perfect opportunity so start your Test career with a very good average, because we won't be staying around here too long."

He was obviously intending to get out very quickly leaving me with a "Not Out" addition to my short Test tally of runs. We had a chat and I encouraged Hoggie to stick around. Then a bit of a partnership started to develop, the runs began to flow and I was beginning to enjoy myself.

But the West Indies were not enjoying the experience which they found frustrating. Malcolm Marshall followed through a bit further than usual after an especially angry delivery.

"Boony, I know you are trying to do the best you can for your country but I am sick to death of you. If you don't get out I am going to come around the wicket and kill you!"

Next over he came around the wicket but I managed to hook one for four. A white-faced Hogg came storming down the wicket, "What the hell do you think you are trying to do? Get us killed!"

Keeping him out in the middle batting with me was one of the most enjoyable moments of my entire career. I am not sure he enjoyed the experience!

Kim Hughes was obviously a skipper under siege but had been extremely welcoming to me. I knew nothing of the traumas that were continuing outside the dressing room as I had a quiet beer with my team mates at the end of the match. Then I looked up to see him enter the rooms and being consoled by some of the other players.

Still the penny did not drop until I heard the word, "quit". A few of the players started looking around the room and then glancing at Allan Border who was sitting beside me. I didn't realise it, but a torrid new era of Australian cricket was about to begin.

Kim remained in the Test team and over the next few days I learned how proud he had been to captain his country and how much it hurt him to resign.

He finished with a captaincy record of four wins, 13 losses and 11 draws. He lost his place in the Test team two matches later, having scored just two runs in his final four innings, including a first ball duck in his last Test innings.

After being left out of the Ashes squad for the 1985 tour to England, he accepted a deal to captain the rebel tour side to South Africa. Hughes believed he had nothing left to offer Australian cricket and was victimised for his association

with the Australian Cricket Board during the World Series Cricket era. Certainly fellow West Australians Rod Marsh and Dennis Lillee made life difficult for him, believing he should not be their captain.

Unfairly, he is remembered more for his unlucky captaincy record and tearful farewell to the captaincy, but was actually one of the most talented batsmen of his generation.

In the First Test in Melbourne against the West Indies in

1981-82, Hughes faced the fearsome fast-bowling quartet of Michael Holding, Colin Croft, Andy Roberts and Joel Garner. His courageous and undefeated century out of a total of only 198 enabled Australia to win a low-scoring match and take a 1-0 lead in the series.

Wisden, in its Top 10 Test Innings of all time, ranked that innings at number 9.

Allan Border

Allan Border didn't want to captain Australia. He did not think he was the right person for the job and did it out of sufferance and his incredible love for the baggy green.

He just wanted to bat for Australia, make runs for Australia, occasionally bowl for Australia and generally enjoy a quiet existence. Even by the end of his career I'm not sure whether he ever really consistently enjoyed the experience of captaining his country.

But there was no one else. Australian cricket was bruised and battered so the stocky left-hander picked up the mantle with his traditional stoicism. He had inherited an inexperienced team and we had very limited self-belief. Adding to his woes, we were only half way through a series against the world champions, the West Indians.

His malaise only became worse when he won the toss in the Fourth Test at the MCG and sent the opposition in to bat. The West Indies immediately compiled a breathtaking 479 with the magnificent Viv Richards dominating with a double century.

We managed to scramble out of the match with a draw – and even that result was some sort of victory for us. The West Indies had won the first three Tests but at least they couldn't make a clean sweep of the series!

Allan Border had been an outstanding teenage cricketer,

playing for his local club, Mosman in 1972 as a 17-year-old. Then he lost interest, turning his back on his bat and preferring the surf at the local beach, where the attractions for a teenage boy were shapelier.

For two seasons he rarely pulled on his creams until the club's captain/coach, Barry Knight, a former English Test all-rounder urged him to give cricket another try.

Knight, at first hand, had seen the fighting abilities of Border in junior teams at Mosman and also admired his batting power through the offside.

The initial devastation of World Series Cricket had selectors throughout Australia searching for promising youngsters to plug holes in State teams. In New South Wales they looked, with the urging of Knight, to Border. Almost immediately their "Hail Mary" scored a century in Perth and a few weeks later was rushed in to the Test team to play England. He was 23 years old and three years earlier had been sunbaking on the beach rather than wielding the willow.

He believed he was unworthy to wear the baggy green and gold cap, but determined to make the best of the situation before the selectors admitted their mistake and returned him to State cricket and then probably park cricket where he felt he belonged.

On that debut day he appeared to be far from enjoying the experience of playing for his country. He made 29 and was then run out for a duck in the second innings but Australia went on to win the game by 103 runs.

The victory ensured his selection for the next Test and his pride and strength of resolve saw him hang around with the tailenders, finishing with an undefeated 60 and 45 in both innings while his team mates fell about beside him like confetti. It was a taste of things to come for the next 15 years of his life.

The young Border danced to the spinners with delicate footwork and even more delicate placement square of the wicket. The short ball was pulled when over-pitched. He could drive fluently with the best.

With the World Series Cricket split mended, he was relieved to see the return of some of the legends of the game and content to drop down the order and continue his career in their shadow.

It was a luxury he enjoyed, averaging 49.75 in the 1979/80 Series against England which Australia won 3-0, and then to Pakistan where he averaged over 130 aided sensationally by legendary performances of 150 not out and 153 at Lahore.

But then came the disastrous 1981 tour of England, which Australia lost 3-1, being completely shell-shocked by Ian Botham. Border was the only batsman to succeed. He finished the series with a 59.22 average. Then the West Indies visited again and he averaged 67.2 against the best fast bowlers in the world. He was now Australia's most successful batsman but his technique had changed as he came to grips with being the stalwart his nation expected.

He no longer danced to the spinners and the hook shot had been eradicated from his repertoire. Instead, he was punishing through point and strong in the arc forward of a wicket. The pull shot remained, but often he was just as happy to see the ball fly past unchallenged.

After helping Australia regain the Ashes in 1982/83 with 317 runs at 45.29, he set off for the next tour of the West Indies defiant and determined.

Now he faced Joel Garner, Wayne Daniel and Malcolm Marshall as the next generation of fast bowlers began to stamp their credentials on the cricket world and also on the chests of opposing batsmen.

Australia lost the series 3-0. Border made more than 500 runs at an average of 74.73 batting within his restricted range of shots, playing powerfully square of the wicket and confidently handling deliveries passing at well above chest height.

Taking over the captaincy and taking the Australian team to England in 1985 was his next daunting challenge. Suddenly he faced the prospect of losing many of his more experienced players to a rebel tour of South Africa. As a first-year-player I can vividly remember sitting beside another new face in Simon O'Donnell as part of an Australian Test team "jury" listening to Test players Wayne Phillips, Murray Bennett, Dirk Welham and Graeme Wood, explaining their stance on South Africa while we decided if they should accompany us on the Ashes tour to England.

It was an excruciating and embarrassing time for all concerned. I don't know why it happened or how it happened; I just know it should not have happened.

In the end common sense prevailed and everyone went on the English tour although again, it was a team split by factions.

I started the tour rooming with the former South African, then Australian, and later South African again Kepler Wessells and answered a very mysterious telephone call for him. It was always said that he was the "fifth columnist" in our ranks. In fact he returned to play cricket in South Africa shortly after.

But to this day I don't know just how closely he was involved in the defection of the Aussies. But I have my suspicions. It was just another challenge that Allan Border had to face and overcome.

In those early years he captained a team that was more like a passing parade of Test hopefuls. In New Zealand when he played his 60th Test, the rest of the team had not totalled 60 Tests between them. Despite his best efforts we showed little

resilience in the last two Tests of the series and he felt the team had not progressed since the 1981 humiliation.

The steely grit was even more pronounced as he showed the cricketing world an unsmiling and grim exterior. Australia was losing, he was bleeding, and there was no room for tolerance. The media pronounced him "Captain Grumpy" and he did nothing to quell their description.

A dreadful tour of Pakistan was followed by the West Indies arriving in Australia. In the Third Test in Melbourne, the Australians were set a target of 404 but we fell disgracefully to be all out for 114. Border was again supreme. He batted for nearly three hours for 20 runs and a pummelling from the West Indian quick bowlers.

"I get absolutely no joy from Test cricket as it has been in this match," he said at the game post match media conference. The media declared him a "one man team" and that pronouncement was emphasised in the next match in Sydney where he provided the spin bowling and surprised by taking 11 for 96 disclosing that the West Indies were vulnerable to the spinning ball.

But the tide was beginning to turn. England in 1989 was a watershed.

We began to mature with opener Mark Taylor averaging 83.9, Steve Waugh a remarkable 126.5 and fast bowlers Terry Alderman and Geoff Lawson picked up 70 wickets between them. It was like a dream. Australia grabbed a 4-0 victory to take the Ashes against the old foe.

Now sweeping all before them the summer of 1990/91 saw us retain the Ashes with a score line of 3-0. Happy in victory, Border still had one mountain to climb and that was the bruising, belligerent West Indians. But it wasn't to be. The West Indies won the first two of the four Test series and although the Aussies won the last Test match, Border's ultimate

ambition had not been fulfilled.

He had another attempt at them in the summer of 1992/93 and aided by the leg spinning sensation, Shane Warne, almost pulled it off. Warne took 7 for 52 at the MCG on the last day of the second Test to give his team victory but the Aussies failed by two runs in Adelaide and then in the pace furnace of Perth we were sliced apart by Curtly Ambrose and Bishop. They took nine and eight wickets respectively for only a handful of runs and we lost the series 1-2.

Back to England and it was Shane Warne and Merv Hughes in full cry. The Ashes were retained 4-1, in time for the skipper's 38th birthday. The man, who had toiled as a solitary light in an otherwise black night for Australian cricket, now had built a successful team around him and as he edged towards his 40th year, it was time to pass the mantle on with grace and a smile. Mission accomplished. No longer was he "Captain Grumpy."

A year after he retired, we won back the Sir Frank Worrell Trophy at Sabina Park and he was there as a cricket commentator and that victory evening left me with mixed emotions.

I was delighted he was at the ground to enjoy the experience and join us in the dressing rooms. But I was depressed that he was not part of the action – a member of the team that had turned the tables after more than a decade of humiliation.

As a captain he was old fashioned, brutally honest and loyal to a fault. He never criticised players in front of their peers, preferring to highlight the team's performance, or lack of it, rather than dumping on individuals (the only exception was at the Oval in 1985 when Andrew Hilditch who is now Chair of the Australian selectors, was dismissed hooking after Border had repeatedly told him to cut it out of his repertoire).

But usually if AB had something to tell you, then he preferred to do it over a beer at the bar or in a quiet spot.

117

I can see remarkable similarities in those that followed him. All took a touch of AB into their leadership position – Mark Taylor, Steve Waugh and Ricky Ponting. All aggressive, up-front leaders and all, I believe, can trace it back to an Allan Border who lifted a dispirited and lost bunch of players to the pinnacle of World cricket.

AB remains and will always be a very close friend, even though I disagreed vehemently with his decision as captain not to allow wives to stay at the team hotel until the end of the 1989 tour.

At least I was one of the team who respected the decision and didn't flaunt it!

We have since walked, talked, selected, golfed together and he continues to serve Australian cricket.

Allan Border led the resurgence of Australian cricket to where it is today.

Mark Taylor

While the media admired Allan Border for his fighting qualities and old fashioned leadership, the arrival of Mark Taylor was like a breath of fresh air for cricket writers and cricket administrators.

A good communicator, his easy going and friendly style made him a "good talent" and immensely popular in the lounge rooms of Australia where his bright and breezy attitude to cricket won the hearts of kids and their mums across the nation.

Taylor first came under notice at the Australian Under 19 Championships in 1984 when he compiled 334 runs, second only to another youngster, Steve Waugh, who scored 387. A precise batsman who tended to construct an innings by placement rather than power, he was just as careful off the field ensuring that he studied for a degree in surveying while

trying to force his way into the New South Wales and Australian teams.

Funnily enough Mark Taylor and Mark Waugh made their Shield debuts together against Tasmania at the old TCA ground. Right from the start there was something about those two!

You knew Mark Taylor was going to make something of himself away from cricket. In years to come I can see him as a member of parliament, probably a Minister. He has got the whole package. Assured, gift of the gab and a remarkable air of confidence.

When Allan Border announced his retirement I was keen for the job. I would have dearly loved to captain Australia, but I was nearing the end of my career and as was explained to me by an ACB representative they were looking for longevity in the next leader because that had been a successful formula in the past. So Mark received the nod and almost immediately proved to be an astute skipper.

He had tremendous leadership skills, was an exceptionally good tactician and had a sharp cricket brain. Also he inherited a good team and that allowed him to be aggressive.

He had an uncanny knack to predict and read a match. He could quickly identify a batsman's weakness or when a change had to be initiated in the field or at the bowling crease.

As a batsman Taylor learned to play to his strengths. One of the funnier moments was when he was obviously getting a fair bit from the opposition at Trent Bridge. Between majestic drives through the covers he toyed with the many movements being made in the slips formation by deft placement of calculated edges past the clutching fieldsmen on his way to a century during that epic partnership with Geoff Marsh.

He was undoubtedly one of Australia's finest captains.

119

His selection for his first Test was against the West Indies in Sydney in January 1989. But his start was hardly the debut of dreams. Curtly Ambrose dismissed him for 25 and three, but Australia did win the match. In the Fifth Test at Adelaide he was run out twice for three and 36 in a draw.

At the end of the summer Taylor had played in two Test matches which Australia had not lost and had survived his baptism of bounce, bumpers and bruising from the West Indians. He was taken on the 1989 Ashes tour with the selectors hoping that he could open the innings with Geoff Marsh, allowing me to bat at number three and hopefully add a touch of solidarity to what many say is the most demanding position in cricket.

The dominoes fell into place and he grabbed his opportunity scoring 136 in his first innings against the traditional foe.

It was a performance that saw him move from careful placement and caressing of the ball through the field to all out aggression on the offside and some smacking pull shots to the fence. He backed up with 60 in the second innings and then a string of scores throughout the rest of the series helping us regain the Ashes by the end of the Fourth Test at Old Trafford with a 3-0 lead.

A belligerent 219 in the next and additional runs (71 and 48 in the final Test) saw him finish the series with an average of 83.9 and an aggregate of 839 runs, placing him second only to the mighty Don Bradman's 1930 record of 974 runs at 139.14. To cap off a wonderful season he was named as one of *Wisden's* Cricketers of the Year.

The fairy tale continued against Sri Lanka and Pakistan as he continued to maintain a Test average in excess of 80 during 12 Tests against three countries in nine months.

In cricket, for every up, there is a down and in the following

year when the English toured Australia, he could only manage 213 runs at 23.67. But in typical style Taylor took it in his stride and prepared himself for his first daunting tour of the Caribbean.

Against the calypso speed kings, he found form again, scoring 442 runs at an average of 49, often taking on the brutal bowling and leading the Aussies from the front – the opener's position.

He had replaced Geoff Lawson as captain of New South Wales and when Geoff Marsh was dropped for the Fifth Test against India in 1991/92, Taylor took over as Border's deputy and heir apparent to the most important job in the nation.

Then the West Indies arrived and this time the barrage proved too much. He could manage only 170 runs at 24.29 in the first four Tests and was dropped to drinks-waiter for the fifth in Perth.

England was looming with the 1993 tour and Taylor, the hero of the previous tour, was determined to visit the "old country" again. He did well enough in New Zealand to make the side, but again once he was on English soil, his bat began belting out scores. Centuries in the first two Tests quickly revitalised his reputation and he compiled 428 runs at an average of 42.8.

As captain his first campaign was to Pakistan where his team struggled. But then in the 1994/95 Ashes Series, he led us to a 3-1 victory and then to the Caribbean.

Where so many before had failed, his team won the series and brought the longest reign in cricket to a close. The West Indies had been undefeated in 29 series over 17 years and under "Tubby" Taylor we achieved what so many had tried and failed.

Australia was now the top Test cricketing nation in the world and Taylor's challenge was to keep us there! Pakistan and

Sri Lanka came and went and then the West Indies were handled 3-2 in the return series. The team was taking all before it, but Taylor, hampered by a back injury, could manage just 153 runs at an average of 17 against the West Indies and his poor run continued in South Africa when he could manage only 80 runs at an average of 16. Only the success of the team saved Taylor's neck.

Then it was off to England again and the Aussie side was soon rocking back on its heels after suffering a 3-0 defeat in the One-Day series.

Taylor was still horribly out of touch and as the First Test loomed only a dropped catch by Dean Jones, who was captaining Derbyshire, allowed Taylor to make 63, and avert the possibility of the skipper not being in the team for the opening of hostilities for the Ashes. Despite his performance with the bat, his popularity knew no bounds. Throughout his run of outs he had remained affable and his leadership remained unflappable.

The public loved him and back in Australia letters in the daily media urged the nation's cricket fans to "pray for our leader."

Looking on after I retired I realised how mentally tough he was – at all times. When he was having his run of small scores and the media was calling for his head his captaincy was still outstanding. His demeanour never waived. He was always polite and upbeat with the media although he must have been suffering internally.

His trick was to deflect all questions to the team rather than Mark Taylor as an individual. As a team leader he never allowed his own run of misfortune cloud his judgement as a skipper. It was spot on and I could never fault his decision-making.

In the first innings at Edgbaston he could manage only

Mate at the crease

I spent most of my education at Launceston Grammar with David Boon. As a direct result it's fair to say that I am not a great scholar.

I don't remember him being caned by deputy principal Trevor Sorell. But he undoubtedly deserved it. He was behind most of the misdemeanours at the school during my years there.

I was a fairly innocent kid but he seemed to drag me into trouble. Perhaps I was easily led.

I can distinctly remember in Year 12 when we were both studying for matriculation. Accounting was beyond us and an automatic fail.

But British History was a different story. All those kings, queens and battles. I was expecting big things but when I sat down in the examination room there he was sitting directly behind me.

Within half an hour of a three-hour examination he slammed down his pen. "Come on, time to go" he whispered.

"No, I want to pass. This is my best subject."

On and on he went. Every five minutes he would hiss, "Come on, time to go. Let's go!"

It was much worse than a hundred Boony Dolls.

"Just a few minutes more," I would plead. "Just finish this question".

"No. Come on, let's go."

This whispering campaign continued until, with 30 minutes of the exam to go, I relented and left the final question half finished. Off we went to have a session in the nets. As always he batted and I bowled.

The result of that exam? Failed by a miserable two marks!

Peter Faulkner
Chairman of Selectors, Tasmanian Cricket Association

seven runs and he went out to bat in the second innings knowing that if he failed then his Test career was over in the most embarrassing circumstances possible.

The pressure was immense, probably immeasurable as the skipper decided to throw caution to the wind. His timing was astray but he went for his shots. Lurching onto his front foot he swiped. Rocking back onto his heels he swatted. He reached 50 in 69 minutes – but there were many edges amongst those runs. By stumps he had scored 108 and went on to finish on 129. It was wonderful to watch.

His performance completely altered the mental state of our team. We lost that Test but the sun was shining again, the "Skip" was in form and we went on to a 3-2 series win.

The next summer the captaincy of the One-Day team was given to Steve Waugh. But series wins against New Zealand and South Africa ensured that Taylor's Midas touch as Test captain continued. However, all good things must come to an end and in 1998 his team toured India and lost 2-1. It brought to an end a nine Test series winning streak under his captaincy which was the best by any Australian team.

Then it was Pakistan in October 1998 and he wanted revenge for the tour loss four years earlier, but again his form deserted him in the First Test. The second clash was at Peshawar and Mark Taylor had a date with destiny. He scored a magnificent 334 not out and declared the Australian innings closed overnight. The magical 334 equalled Don Bradman's famous innings – the highest Test score by an Australian. Only one more run and the crown was Taylor's.

His unselfish decision not to continue batting the next morning in the best interests of a team pursuing victory lifted him from being an extremely popular cricket captain to folk hero status back in Australia. He was inundated with offers for

TV advertisements, endorsements and sponsorships.

His fantastic innings was followed by a 92 in the second innings and he was again at his batting pinnacle. But Father Time waits for no man and while he captained his team to victory in the Ashes the following summer in Australia, his form again was wasting away.

Taylor was named Australian of the Year early in 1999 and shortly after announced his retirement from the Test arena. He had played in 104 Tests and scored 7,525 runs at an average of 43.49. He had also taken 157 catches as one of the nation's best ever slips fieldsmen. He retired as undoubtedly Australia's most popular captain for 50 years. A folk hero to a nation.

Steve Waugh

When Steve Waugh took over the Australian captaincy in February 1999, it was like a step back into the future for cricket fans.

Gone was the affable Mark Taylor who suffered stoically over his long run of bad form and always managed to pump up his team whatever the circumstances. Instead, Steve Waugh reminded many of Allan Border. He appeared dark and brooding. A difficult man to welcome into the lounge rooms of Australia.

In fact to Steve cricket was always a battle. It was a war of attrition that had to be fought on an eyeball to eyeball basis. More than any other of our recent captains he grew enormously with the job.

He was perceived as having a deficiency against short and fast bowling. So he worked on countering the weakness. He became a minimum risk player by cutting out shots that put his wicket unduly in danger.

He restricted his range of shots making the opposition

bowl to his strengths. The hook and the pull were discarded and he manufactured that short arm "Bludgeon" through the onside.

As a cricketer he was a traditionalist, took pride in the history of cricket, was single minded and at times blinkered in his view of what to do and who would do it. You could be mistaken for thinking he was from a previous era. But the word respect is the word you associate with Steve Waugh.

He achieved through perseverance and learned from those who had gone before. He had the up front leadership of Allan Border and the tactical mind of Taylor.

But for Steve Waugh there was no option but winning and as a result he was always positive and aggressive.

Like Allan Border he could always get the best out of the tail end batsmen. Some of Australia's greatest efforts were with Steve leading the tail to achieve great things with the bat. He had faith in them and would chat with them after every over – sometimes every ball – pumping up their confidence, and it worked.

His career as captain certainly didn't start well against the West Indies in the Caribbean. Brian Lara was at his peak and no one, especially, Waugh knew how to contain him. The tourists scraped in for a 2/2 drawn series and a skipper relieved he had not handed the Sir Frank Worrell Trophy back to the Windies.

Then it was on to the 1999 World Cup in England. Australia looked certain to be out of the tournament early after a string of lack lustre performances. But Waugh, determined and defensive at media conferences, would not be deterred. At no stage did he agree Australia couldn't make the final – even when the Aussies had to win seven games on end to take the Cup. No one but his team mates believed him.

But it was Waugh who lifted his team into the final. Against South Africa in the fifth of those seven games, he hit

120 not out to give his team a sniff of victory. In more than 200 previous One-Day matches for his nation he had scored only a solitary century. On this occasion he was "last man standing" as his fellow batsmen toppled around him. Australia won the match and then thrashed Pakistan to take the Cup.

Steve Waugh's self-belief had been justified and his team believed that he was some sort of Messiah as he led them by example through the coming months.

From November 1999 until April 2000 Australia was to play Test matches against Pakistan, India and New Zealand. Waugh said publicly that he believed the Aussies could win each match and his optimism was endemic amongst his team mates.

In Hobart in the Second Test against Pakistan, Adam Gilchrist and Justin Langer had to chase down 369 runs to keep Waugh's dream alive.

Sure enough, Waugh's crystal ball gazing prophecy of a clean sweep became a fact and Waugh, never one of Australia's most loved captains, was now one of the most respected.

His team played matches not day-by-day, but session by session. Psychologically they destroyed the opposition by putting selective targets under verbal attack on the field. And of course with success came a softening of the hard-edged image. He was now more relaxed at media conferences, although quick to take offence at any criticism of his team.

His performance in his first 12 months as captain saw him tear up the record books with 12 wins, three losses and two draws in 17 games. This placed him ahead of even the great Don Bradman in captaincy results.

Eventually his ruthless approach led to a run of 16 consecutive Test match victories, obliterating the previous record of 11 by the West Indies.

He captained Australia on 57 occasions and led them to 41

victories – the most of any Test captain.

After playing in nine successive Ashes Series the 2002/2003 Series was his last against the traditional foe and supplied cricket fans with an unforgettable memory.

For quite some time Waugh had been receiving some heavy criticism from the media because of his advancing years and lack of form. The selectors had been monitoring the situation and discussing the future with him for some time, even though this position was not always accurately portrayed in the media.

He deserved respect and some leeway and he certainly had our support as selectors. With this weight on his shoulders he came to the wicket with the hopes and hearts of Australia firmly behind him.

In a remarkable display of determination he spent the second afternoon of the match scoring a chanceless century with his trademark "slog sweep" against the spinners proving effective to the delight and delirium of the crowd.

Entering the final over of the day on 97 he smacked a boundary through cover point off the last ball of the day to bring up his century and save his Test career.

He retired from international cricket and the captaincy after the Fourth Test against India in January 2004. But not before he played a typical gutsy final Test innings, compiling his highest fourth innings score of 80 on the final day of the Test to save Australia from the ignominy of their first home series defeat in 12 years.

As he passed 50 the applause from the crowd was supported by the rare sound of all the Sydney Harbour ferries sounding their horns in acknowledgement of the retiring champion.

An all time record number of fans also turned out on the fifth day to bid him farewell.

Ricky Ponting

The current captain of the Australian One-Day and Test cricket teams he heads into the Ashes Series with plenty to prove – and disprove!

He is the world's leading Test batsman according to ICC rankings and second in the One-Day rankings. He has made over 8,500 Test runs in 103 Tests at an average of over 58 with 31 centuries.

In One-Day international matches Ponting has made more than 9,000 runs in 2,509 matches at an average of 42.

A proud record for a man whose pride was sorely dented when he led his side to defeat against the English to lose the 2005 Ashes. Only recovering the little urn will satisfy him, his team mates and the nation!

Ponting is a prodigious leader and has grown, despite some rude lessons, under the mantle of leadership. His captaincy has improved. It's sharper, more instinctive and he is prepared to take risks by taking the initiative.

But life in cricket has been a roller coaster.

He started as a Shield player at 17, Test player at 20 and immediately scoring 96 before a shocking LBW decision ended his hopes of a debut century. Then dropped after six Tests but back again for Leeds and his first Test century.

Last season he scored a century in both innings of a Test match on three occasions – the first player to achieve the feat in a single season. He is also the only cricketer to win the Allan Border medal twice and the only batsman to twice score over 1500 Test match runs in a calendar year.

As a captain he is a traditionalist like Steve Waugh, aggressive like Mark Taylor and leading from the front in the manner of Allan Border.

Certainly the Ashes were not so successful. Dismissed three

times in single figures before he scored 156 at Old Trafford to rescue his nation – the first Test century of the series.

At Edgbaston his whole captaincy came under intense review and discussion in the media. He won the toss asked England to bat and threw the gauntlet down to his bowlers.

The fact was that the bowlers didn't perform well enough but he copped the criticism, which rests with the captain. Some say it was the decision that lost the Ashes. I don't think so. We

just didn't play well enough.

He has tremendous belief in his players and it was one of the few times it wasn't reciprocated.

At Trent Bridge he had scored a well-compiled 48 before being brilliantly run out by young substitute English fielder Gary Pratt.

The excessive use of substitute fieldsmen in the series by the less than agile opposition had angered the Aussie captain and his tirade of abuse at the English balcony as he left the field cost him 75% of his match fee, and some say, let England know that the Australians were rattled.

Since the Ashes his batting has reached new heights. Given the captaincy many players find their form plateaus. Ponting's form during the past 12 months has secured his position as currently the world's greatest batsman.

Since returning from their unsuccessful Ashes campaign in England, Australia has won 11 and drawn one of 12 Tests and won 18 of 25 One-Day internationals.

We all learn from our experiences and hasn't the cricket world paid since. Certainly the South Africans had a real taste of Ponting. He scored a century in each innings of the third and final Test against them at the Sydney Cricket Ground over the New Year period.

Then he scored his magnificent 164 in the record-breaking one-day international at the Wanderers. At Newlands he scored 74 in the first innings. At Kingsmead he went one better, scoring a century in each innings of the Second Test against a demoralised South African bowling attack.

When he reached his century a week later in the Third Test, Ponting joined India's Sunil Gavaskar as the only players in cricket history to score a century in each innings of a Test on three occasions. A remarkable effort.

131

He first did it against the West Indies at the Gabba in Brisbane on the occasion of his 100th Test for Australia. Ponting made 1,544 in 15 Tests in the 2005 calendar year, the second highest number of runs after West Indian legend Viv Richards, who made 1,710 in 11 Tests in 1976. It included a brilliant 118 not out to save Australia from an embarrassing loss to Bangladesh – reinforcing the belief Ponting is behind only Don Bradman as our greatest batsman.

The brilliant Ponting now has 8,740 runs in Test cricket, if he plays another nine years and into his 40's, as predicted by some, he could conceivably double his run count, pushing him well past the 16,000 mark.

Sixteen Australians have played Test cricket into their 40s. Bob Simpson was the last, playing his final Test at the age of 42 in May 1978, after making a comeback to help the establishment team during World Series Cricket.

As with all cricket captains they are leaders of men and Ponting, in my opinion, is going to be one of the best.

1985

My first tour was a learning process, unfortunately. I made a lot of runs in county cricket but went hungry in the three Test matches I played. It was a difficult time but a wonderful educational experience. I was new in the team, not doing all that well with the bat and the rebel tour by many of our team mates was looming.

The legendary Jeff Thomson was a revelation to this young tourist. Whenever we were flat, often on a long bus trip, he would lift our spirits with an array of jokes and far fetched stories.

I made a lifetime mate in Murray Bennett and after the tour we took our wives on a wonderful holiday in the Greek Isles. Friendship, one of the greatest things you can gain from cricket.

1985 – HEADINGLY – FIRST TEST
June 13, 14, 15, 17, 18
AUSTRALIA 331 (*Hilditch 119, Ritchie 46*) and 324 (*Phillips 91, Hilditch 80, Wessels 64, Emburey 5 for 82, Botham 4 for 107*) ENGLAND 533 (*Robinson 175, Botham 60, Downton 54, Gatting 53, McDermott 4 for 134*) and 5 for 123
England won by 5 wickets

England was strengthened by the return of Graham Gooch and John Emburey after a three-year ban for touring South Africa and they certainly got away to a strong start in their quest to regain the Ashes.

The unheard of Tim Robinson from Notts made 175, which was the second highest score in a debut innings in the Ashes Series.

He was at the crease for seven hours, facing Craig

McDermott, Simon O'Donnell, Jeff Thomson, and Geoff Lawson. It was an amazing performance which even outshone Ian Botham, at his bruising best, pounding 60 runs off 51 balls to give England a first innings lead of 202 and the country's highest total ever against Australia at Leeds.

Poor Jeff Thomson conceded a record 166 runs which was more than any other Australian fast bowler in a Test innings. After an outstanding 91 from Australian wicket-keeper, Wayne Phillips, England needed 123 in 200 minutes to win the match in overcast and threatening weather.

Lawson and O'Donnell had England 4/83 but England was up to the challenge and won by five wickets. Apart from his 60 which included 10 fours and a six, Botham took three wickets in four balls in the first innings. It was a stark reminder to us that he was still a powerhouse of English cricket.

1985 – LORD'S – SECOND TEST
June 27, 28, 29, July 1, 2
ENGLAND 290 (Gower 86, Lamb 47, McDermott 6 for 70) and 261 (Botham 85, Gatting 75, Holland 5 for 68)
AUSTRALIA 425 (Border 196, Ritchie 94, O'Donnell 48, Botham 5 for 109 and 6 for 127 (Border 41)
Australia won by 4 wickets

I had been there before, in 1978, but to play for Australia at the home of cricket is a dream. It was surreal that first time as I walked into the ground, into the dressing room and finally out onto the turf where you could almost feel the ghosts of the famous names who had walked before you.

This was Allan Border's match. He scored 196 in seven and a half hours which was the highest by an Australian captain on this ground. In the second innings when Australia was teetering,

he scored a gritty 41 not out to ensure victory.

Australia went into the match with only four main bowlers but pulled off the nation's 10th victory at Lord's to level the series.

Border eventually fell to Ian Botham giving "Both" his 25th five-wicket haul in a Test innings while Border reached 5,000 Test runs in a record time of six years and 186 days.

In fact he should have been out at 87 when he flipped the ball to Mike Gatting at short square leg, but the fieldsman accidentally tossed the ball away in his eagerness to celebrate taking a superb catch.

The bowling hero for the Aussies was Bob "Dutchy" Holland, the 38-year-old grey haired leg spinner who finished with 5/68. One of the game's gentlemen.

In three Tests at Lord's I had not been part of a losing team but thankfully the next two were to be more personally successful than this one.

1985 – TRENT BRIDGE – THIRD TEST
July 11, 12, 13, 15, 16
ENGLAND 456 (*Gower 166, Gatting 74, Gooch 70, Lawson 5 for 103*) and 2 for 196 (*Robinson 77, Gooch 48*)
AUSTRALIA 539 (*Wood 172, Ritchie 146, Hilditch 47, O'Donnell 46*)
Match drawn

This match was drawn due to rain and a classic wicket. The undoubted highlight was David Gower's 166 which for me was a study in nonchalant elegance. For Australia, Graeme Wood's 172 and Greg Ritchie's 146 resurrected their careers and the match was a solid foundation for Australian batting yet to come.

1985 – OLD TRAFFORD – FOURTH TEST

August 1, 2, 3, 5, 6

AUSTRALIA 257 *(Boon 61, Hilditch 49, O'Donnell 45, Edmonds 4 for 40, Botham 4 for 79)* and 5 for 340 *(Border 146, Wessels 50, Hilditch 40, Emburey 4 for 99)*

ENGLAND 9 for 482 declared *(Gatting 160, Gooch 74, Lamb 67, Gower 47, McDermott 8 for 141)*

Match drawn

Another drawn match due to the weather. Australia, invited to bat by Gower, struggled to 257. I managed my highest Test score of 61, batting at number three. Botham caused me quite a few headaches with sone snarling deliveries – off his short run! England scored almost 500 runs in response with Gatting proving he could bat with 160, but for cricket buffs the undoubted highlight was Craig McDermott, at 20 years and 114 days, becoming the youngest to take eight wickets in an innings of an Ashes Test. It seemed the replacement for Dennis Lillee had arrived.

Australia's hero was yet again Allan Border who rescued the team from four for 138 – still 87 runs behind.

He batted throughout the final day in a dark concentration that reflected the weather. He made an unbeaten 146 to ensure that Australia would live to fight another day.

1985 – EDGBASTON – FIFTH TEST

August 15, 16, 17, 19, 20

AUSTRALIA 335 *(Wessels 83, Lawson 53, Border 45, Ellison 6 for 77)* and 142 *(Phillips 59, Ellison 4 for 27)*

ENGLAND 5 for 595 declared *(Gower 215, Robinson 148, Gatting 100, Lamb 46)*

England won by an innings and 118 runs

The adventurous Gower became the first English captain to put Australia into bat in consecutive Tests, and when the Aussies scored 335 it appeared as if his gamble may have backfired. Then Gower made amends for his possible error by scoring a double century, and in partnership with the unheralded Robinson, who scored 148, their second wicket partnership of 331 put them well on the way to a victory.

To add insult to injury, when Botham came to the wicket, he hit the first and third balls he received from McDermott for six, his way to quell the debate about whether McDermott would ever become the second Dennis Lillee. Thankfully there has only ever been one "Beefy" and he did everything with a flourish. Australia collapsed when we visited the crease again with the first five wickets tumbling for 36 runs, the invaluable wicket of Border being among them. It was an extremely disappointing performance.

1985 – THE OVAL – SIXTH TEST
August 29, 30, 31, September 2
ENGLAND 464 (Gooch 196, Gower 157, Lawson 4 for 101, McDermott 4 for 108)
AUSTRALIA 241 (Ritchie 64) and 129 (Border 58, Ellison 5 for 46)
England won by an innings and 94 runs

England continued its hunger for runs, scoring 464 with Graham Gooch four runs short of a double century and Gower continuing his superlative form. In fact, apart from being Gooch's highest Test score and his first century against Australia after 40 attempts, the Gower/Gooch second wicket stand was a massive 351. So in the matter of only a few weeks, the second and third highest stands by England in 108 years and more than

a century of Ashes matches, had been set.

Australia collapsed twice with Border the only player showing any semblance of resistance in the second innings making 58, taking his total in the series to 597 runs. All of them in typical fighting mood. He let the rest of us know that our performances were not up to scratch. Although personally in form he was not enjoying his cricket.

This series lit a fire in my belly that would sustain me through Australia's rebuilding period. It was the start of my own personal battle with the English and the start of some great friendships.

1986/87

This was a summer I was determined to show that I could play! But it was either a feast or a famine. I either belted a century or out for a duck. I became dreadfully indecisive and developed a bad case of the "yips". My footwork was gone, my shot selection deplorable and my confidence in tatters. The selectors had no choice. I was dropped and two days after the Third Test was playing for Tasmania against Queensland.

Craig McDermott had been dropped as well and sure enough I gently gloved him behind the wicket when I was on seven. I thought it was a career defining moment as I trudged back to the pavilion and spent a sleepless night contemplating my future. Sports psychologist and former West Indian fast bowler Rudi Webster in his book *Winning Ways* wrote that all players have bad times. You never lose your talent – it just goes missing.

You will never improve until you admit you are at rock bottom, Sir Garfield Sobers said in the book.

Well I was there. The second innings against Queensland was looming and I was shaking. In the middle the feet were again

moving slowly and the hands! I decided just to play my shots. Play by intuition and enjoy myself. Five hours and 180 runs later my career was on track again.

The difference between success and failure is so close.

1986/87 – BRISBANE – FIRST TEST
November 14, 15, 16, 18, 19
ENGLAND 456 *(Botham 138, Athey 76, Gatting 61, Gower 51, Lamb 40, DeFreitas 40)* and 3 for 77
AUSTRALIA 248 *(Marsh 56, Matthews 56, Ritchie 41, Dilley 5 for 68)* and 282 *(Marsh 110, Ritchie 45, Emburey 5 for 80)*
England won by 7 wickets

Australia went into the series confident that our new look team had England's measure. But immediately there was a feeling of déjà vu as Ian Botham immediately set about our bowlers hitting 138 runs off 174 balls including 13 fours and four huge sixes. Botham belted Merv Hughes for 22 runs off one over. I can recall Merv asking me where he should bowl.

"Why not try some line and length!" The next ball went for six. So much for my help. For Australia Geoff Marsh, Greg Matthews and Ritchie all showed some fight during the match that proved an easy victory for England.

1986/87 – PERTH – SECOND TEST
November 28, 29, 30, December 2, 3
ENGLAND 8 for 592 declared *(Broad 162, Gower 136, Richards 133, Athey 96, Reid 4 for 115)* and 199 for 8 declared *(Gatting 70, Gower 48, S. Waugh 5 for 69)*
AUSTRALIA 401 *(Border 125, S. Waugh 71, Matthews 45, Dilley 4 for 79)* and 4 for 197 *(Jones 69, Marsh 49)*
Match drawn

We were always on the back foot in this match. England compiled 8 declared for 592, their second highest score in Australia behind 636 in Sydney back on the 1928/29 tour. The highlight for Australia was the bowling of lanky Bruce Reid, who grabbed four wickets in the first innings and the batting of Allan Border. He scored his 20th century which took him six hours and was yet another typical batting cameo. He batted with the tail-end and their efforts averted the follow-on and Australia was half way to saving the match.

England's declaration left Australia 391 to make on the final day. It was never an option, despite Botham disappearing from the bowling crease due to a torn chest muscle, as Dean Jones and Graham Marsh guided Australia to the safety of a draw.

1986/87 – ADELAIDE – THIRD TEST
December 12, 13, 14, 15, 16
AUSTRALIA 5 for 514 declared *(Boon 103, Jones 93, S. Waugh 79, Matthews 73, Border 70, Marsh 43)* and 3 for 201 declared *(Border 100, Ritchie 46, Marsh 41)*
ENGLAND 455 *(Broad 116, Gatting 100, Athey 55, Emburey 49, Reid 4 for 64, Sleep 4 for 132)* and 2 for 39
Match drawn

Adelaide was another run feast.

Without the injured Botham, England had only four front line bowlers and I enjoyed their discomfort, finally breaking through against England for a century.

It took four and a half hours and for much of the time I was partnered by Dean Jones who helped me concentrate on the job at hand. Jones was unlucky not to make a century as Australia rushed past 500 before declaring. England's response was just as stoic with Australian leg spinner, Peter Sleep, playing in front of

Right: Man-of-the-Match. *Nikhil Bhattacharya Photography*

his home crowd, sending down 47 overs to take 4/132.

1986/87 – MELBOURNE – FOURTH TEST
December 26, 27, 28
AUSTRALIA 141 (*Jones 59, Botham 5 for 41, Small 5 for 48*)
and 194 (*Marsh 60, S. Waugh 49*)
ENGLAND 349 (*Broad 112, Lamb 43, Gatting 40, Reid 4 for 78, McDermott 4 for 83*)
England won by an innings and 14 runs

The match was a disaster for Australia. Unmitigated! Dismissed in the first innings on the first day for 141, there were few redeeming features. Ian Botham, still suffering from a chest injury, bowled half pace to take five wickets while Gladstone Small, making his debut for England in an Ashes match, also grabbed five scalps.

Due to injuries Gladstone Small and Phillip DeFreitas made up a West Indian born opening attack for England. The English fieldsmen held every catch and wicketkeeper, Jack Richards, equalled the record five dismissals against Australia by predecessors, Jim Parks and Bob Taylor.

The Australian attack, including McDermott, Hughes and Reid, struggled yet again against Chris Broad, Bill Athey and Mike Gatting with Broad reaching his third century in three Tests. In the final innings we capitulated for 194 with only Marsh, Border and Waugh staying at the crease for any length of time. Ashes lost and again AB's words left us with red ears!

1986/87 – SYDNEY – FIFTH TEST
January 10, 11, 12, 14, 15
AUSTRALIA 343 (*Jones 184, Small 5 for 75*) and 251
(*S. Waugh 73, Border 49, Taylor 42, Emburey 7 for 78*)
ENGLAND 275 (*Gower 72, Emburey 69, Richards 46, Taylor 6
for 78*) and 264 (*Gatting 96, Sleep 5 for 72*)
Australia won by 55 runs

With the fate of the Ashes decided, Australia found form for our first victory in 15 Tests.

The match was highly entertaining even from the selection table where a little known Peter Taylor, a 30 year old off spinner who had only played six first class matches, was selected by the Aussies. Initially, the media thought that the promising New South Wales' batsman, Mark Taylor, had been chosen and that the selectors had made a spelling mistake! In fact the man who was to one day captain Australia was about to be interviewed on television when the mix-up was discovered.

Australia batted first and the highlight was an unbeaten 184 by that effervescent Victorian, Dean Jones.

This was achieved despite an apparent caught behind when he had made only five runs and everyone at the ground, including his batting partner, thought he was out. It only takes one umpire to prove everyone wrong. John Emburey also dropped him at eight. No other batsman scored with the next best batting performance coming from Border.

Hughes and Reid had England reeling at 3/17 until Gower came in to score a sublime 72 including four boundaries – each of them memorable – off a Reid over.

New spin bowler, Peter Taylor, claimed the scalps of Lamb, Botham, Gower, Edmonds, Emburey and Small and at that stage

thought Test cricket was a fairly easy game.

England fought back to have us 5/115 but a crucial stumping miss when Steve Waugh was only 15 was costly. He went on to score 73 and in a partnership with Peter Taylor (how easy is Test cricket?) they scored 98 to point their nation towards a redeeming victory.

But the Englishmen were not to be denied. In the final innings with 20 overs left to play, they were 90 runs from victory and five wickets down. It came down to the last two overs and Australia one wicket away from destiny. Border stuck with spinner Peter Sleep, preferring him to the quicks, but it was not until his final ball that he repaid the captain's confidence, bowling Emburey to give Australia a 55-run victory.

It has always stumped me that in those days no matter how badly we were going, we always did well in Sydney and often won. State teams dreaded going there to play NSW but under the baggy green we felt at home.

I have always loved playing there, which is reflected in my performances. To me it's Australia's version of Lord's.

BICENTENNIAL TEST

I had been brought back for a One-Day Series in Dubai then struggled against Pakistan in a three Test Series. I was in the team but only just. So when the Bicentennial Test was played my future career was again being discussed. It was the only time I ever put myself ahead of the team. I made 12 in the first innings and when Australia was forced to follow-on, I knew my career was on the line. Late on the fourth day I went out to bat and was still there when the match was drawn 24 hours later – 184 not out. I had dispelled the devils – including the web that Phil Emburey had spun over my batting for two years. In my mind I truly belonged!

BICENTENNIAL TEST 1987/88 – SYDNEY

January 29, 30, 31, February 1, 2

ENGLAND 425 (*Broad 139, French 47, Robinson 43, Moxon 40, Taylor 4 for 84*)

AUSTRALIA 214 (*Jones 56, Sleep 41*) **and 2 for 328** (*Boon 184, Marsh 56, Border 48*)

Match drawn

This Test match had been scheduled as part of the nation's celebration of 200 years of white settlement, but any cricket skills learned over those years seemed forgotten as the Australians dropped three catches before lunch.

Chris Broad scored yet another century against us – his fourth in five Tests. We were sick of him. Gatting scored his 13 runs in almost two hours. The crowd was sick of him!

The highlight was Broad's dismissal. A short ball from Waugh bounced off his chest and into the stumps after a seven-hour stay at the crease.

So disgusted with his dismissal, Broad swung his bat into the stumps in a "hissy fit" and was booed from the ground.

Australia continued to drop catches as England's score mounted over 400. Then it was the Aussie's turn. We lost seven wickets in two sessions and were forced to follow-on 211 runs behind.

My career and Australia's fate in the Test was on the line as I marched out late in the afternoon of the fourth day.

I was still there at stumps on the final day of the match, unconquered on 184 to be voted Man of the Match. In *The Australian* newspaper cricket writer Mike Coward wrote that I had "saved Australia from an embarrassing defeat and had secured his future in the Australian team."

It was one of the few times my parents came into the dressing room. We were all bursting with pride. A moment to be treasured as dad, mum and I sat in front of the media.

1989

Success in the World Cup in 1987, salvaging my career at the Bicentennial Test and now a tour of England with the Ashes up for grabs. Life was great. It was a great touring team and one of the really great cricket units. There were no factions within the team like in 1985 and we all had the same ambition – to win the Ashes! The team was extremely stable and even the players

Above: Clarrie & Lesley Boon in the Australian dressing room after the Sydney Bicentennial Test 1988.

who never played a Test, like Tim Zoehrer and Tom Moody, were fantastic team members.

The scene was set at Headingly when AB won the toss. "We will bat," he said with the conditions favouring the bowlers and historically everyone preferring to bowl on what can be a treacherous track on the first day. David Gower almost fell over thinking AB had gone mad. We made over 600 and never looked back.

This was the tour when AB controversially banned wives until the end of the tour. Were they the common denominator for our demise on previous Ashes tours?

1989 – HEADINGLY – FIRST TEST
June 8, 9, 10, 12, 13
AUSTRALIA 7 for 601 declared (*S. Waugh 177, Taylor 136, Jones 79, Hughes 71, Border 66*) and 3 for 230 declared (*Taylor 60, Border 60, Boon 43, Jones 40*)
ENGLAND 430 (*Lamb 125, Barnett 80, Smith 66, Alderman 5 for 107*) and 191 (*Gooch 68, Alderman 5 for 44*)
Australia won by 210 runs

Again, Australia sent its "worst team ever" to England for this Ashes Series, according to the English media. And I was part of it.

Mark Taylor, the batsman, was now in the team and became the 16th Australian to make a century on debut against England. Steve Waugh also scored his first ton. Even Merv Hughes made 71 and Australia was in the luxurious position of declaring on reaching 600 runs.

Without the injured Botham and Gatting, England's batting looked fragile but they managed 430 to avoid the follow-on with a marvellous century by Alan Lamb which was highlighted by more fours than any previous century in an Ashes Test!

The highlight for us was the return of swing king, Terry Alderman, who took five wickets in both innings and although not as lethal as before his dreadful shoulder injury, brought back memories of his 1981 tour success.

1989 – LORD'S – SECOND TEST
June 22, 23, 24, 26, 27
ENGLAND 286 (*Russell 64, Gooch 60, Gower 57, Hughes 4 for 71*) and 359 (*Gower 106, Smith 96, Alderman 6 for 128*)
AUSTRALIA 528 (*S. Waugh 152, Boon 94, Lawson 74, Taylor 62, Emburey 4 for 88*) and 4 for 119 (*Boon 58*)
Australia won by 6 wickets

Leg spinner, Trevor Hohns, who would later become Chairman of Selectors and lead Australia through its most powerful cricketing period, came in for my fellow Tasmanian Greg Campbell, the project player who would hopefully take over from Alderman when he retired.

The Alderman magic of the First Test continued with nine wickets in the match. England, not for the last time, began to feel and see the steely grit of Steve Waugh as he compiled a powerful but undefeated 152. I stupidly fell six runs short of a tantalising century at the home of cricket, but my performance cemented my baggy green on my head as Australia took a stranglehold on the match.

David Gower scored yet another, oh so elegant, century in his characteristic style. Finally the Aussies needed 118 to win and at 4/67 there were nerves a-plenty in the dressing room, and memories of fourth innings collapses abounded around Australia.

The Australian superstition of not moving from your seat or changing the makeup of the room when a tight finish was being fought resulted in Allan Border, who had taken a quick shower after being dismissed, not being allowed back into the room and being forced to wander around out the back of the dressing room until we made the necessary runs.

But then Steve Waugh joined me and his winning boundary took his series aggregate to 350 without being dismissed. I remained not out and extremely content on 58 while somewhere in the back of the pavilion Border became the only Australian captain to twice taste victory at Lord's.

It was a great day only marred by officialdom.

I hadn't seen my 18-month-old daughter Georgie for some time and, after a screaming welcome, my wife suggested I take her up to the dressing room for a drink and show her off to the players.

Unfortunately the doorman wouldn't allow her to enter because she was a female. You can imagine the response from an estranged and enraged father. The doorman is still there today and we laugh about it on my visits to Lord's but at the time it was no laughing matter.

1989 – EDGBASTON – THIRD TEST
July 6, 7, 8, 10, 11
AUSTRALIA 424 (*Jones 157, Taylor 43, S. Waugh 43, Marsh 42, Hohns 40, Fraser 4 for 63*) and 2 for 158 (*Taylor 51, Marsh 42*)
ENGLAND 242 (*Botham 46, Russell 42, Curtis 41*)
Match drawn

English weather, which sliced more than 10 hours from the match, undoubtedly cost us victory against an English team which had Ian Botham back after spinal surgery and Chris Tavaré in the side after five years in the wilderness.

Again Geoff Marsh and Mark Taylor gave Australia a solid start, and a fourth wicket stand of 96 between Dean Jones and myself set the scene for Australia to pass the 400 mark yet again.

The score may have been greater, but a straight drive by Jones clipped the bowler's finger on the way past and ran me out – a shocking way to be dismissed. Some of us still think it was deliberate!

Angus Fraser made his debut for England and was the pick of their attack with 4/53 in the first innings. England could manage only 242 with Botham the only bright light with 46 runs. However they did narrowly avoid the follow-on, effectively forcing the match to be a draw.

1989 – OLD TRAFFORD – FOURTH TEST

July 27, 28, 29, 31, August 1
ENGLAND 260 (*Smith 143, Lawson 6 for 72*) and 264 (*Russell 128, Emburey 64, Alderman 5 for 66*)
AUSTRALIA 447 (*S. Waugh 92, Taylor 85, Border 80, Jones 69, Marsh 47*) and 1 for 81
Australia won by 9 wickets

We won back the Ashes with another resounding victory. Not since 1934 had the Ashes been regained on English soil and it was a moment to savour.

Only Robin Smith put up any show of batting prowess in the first innings, scoring more than half of England's total.

Marsh and Taylor proving an effective opening duo got our innings going with a partnership of 135 but at 3/154, the match was an open book. Then Border came to the crease and along with Jones put Australia on the way to a solid score. Waugh tormented the English and was only eight runs short of yet another century before pulling Angus Fraser to be caught on the boundary at backward square leg.

England responded to be 6/59 with Tim Curtis falling to "yet another brilliant Boon bat pad catch," according to the *Daily Telegraph*. They just kept finding my hands.

Then England's tail wagged and an Australian victory started becoming less certain.

Wicket-keeper, Jack Russell, concentrated on occupying the crease along with a determined John Emburey. Their seventh wicket stand of 142 was an Ashes record at Old Trafford. When Emburey departed, Russell batted on, gaining support from Neil Foster and Angus Fraser. He was at the crease for six hours and if one or two upper order batsmen had shown as much determination, the result may have been different.

His performance left Australia 78 to win the Ashes. Marsh and Taylor started proceedings with yet another solid opening combination, but undeservedly it fell to an extremely ungainly sweep by me for the winning boundary that heralded the rebirth of Australian cricket.

With the winning runs imminent I made an offer to AB, "Mate, you deserve to be out there and score the winning runs. Why don't you go in at three?"

In typical fashion he replied, "No you deserve it just as much. Just get out there and do it yourself." Merv Hughes might have been accustomed to cuddling blokes but it was my first experience when Tubby gave me the Taylor bear hug after we won.

1989 – TRENT BRIDGE – FIFTH TEST
August 10, 11, 12, 14
AUSTRALIA 6 for 602 declared (*Taylor 219, Marsh 138, Boon 73, Border 65*)
ENGLAND 255 (*Smith 101, Alderman 5 for 69*) and 167 (*Atherton 47*)
Australia won by an innings and 180 runs

The English summer just got better for us.

The winning victory at Nottingham was the biggest margin ever inflicted by Australia in England. It started yet again with Marsh and Taylor who both made their highest Test scores in an opening stand of 329.

They batted throughout the first day of the match and well into the second. For that entire period I sat with his pads on in the pavilion. I finally made my way to the wicket 20 minutes before lunch with my team mate's advice ringing in my ears: "After a long partnership you know what happens to the next bloke who goes out to bat."

Suddenly the ball started moving around and batting was an absolute nightmare. Quite amazing!

I struggled through to lunch without making a run and then began to build an innings.

When we lost our first wicket just before lunch on that second day David Gower was asked by a senior English official why he was having a glass of champagne with his lunch. He replied that he was celebrating the wicket.

At one stage Australia was 2/502 and every batsman had made runs except the all-conquering Steve Waugh who was out for a duck!

There were even 61 extras which was a new Ashes record.

Then England had to face Terry Alderman and in conditions that suited swing, he proved extremely difficult as England fell to 4/37, to finally finish at 255 with Alderman again bagging another five wickets.

Forced to follow-on, the disheartened English were all out for 167, giving the Aussies a victory by an innings and 180 runs with a day to spare, and mirroring Don Bradman's 1948 performance of winning four Tests in the series.

1989 – THE OVAL – SIXTH TEST
August 24, 25, 26, 28, 29
AUSTRALIA 468 (*Jones 122, Border 76, Taylor 71, Boon 46, Healy 44, Pringle 4 for 70*) and 4 for 219 declared. (*Border 51, Jones 50, Taylor 48*)
ENGLAND 285 (*Gower 79, Small 59, Alderman 5 for 66*) and 5 for 143 (*Smith 77*)
Match drawn

Again we rocketed past 400 in our first innings for the eighth successive time – a new Test cricket record.

Above: A salute for my highest score, 200. Australia vs New Zealand 1989. *Gregg Porteous Photography.*

Jones scored another typical century, Border yet another half century and Taylor's 71 meant that he had passed 50 for the seventh time in the series and finished with an aggregate of 839 runs at an average of 83.9.

England, with their tail again wagging, made 285 to ensure that we had to put on the pads once more.

It enabled Waugh to pass 500 for the series, as Taylor and Jones had already achieved, meaning that three batsmen passing that total was yet another Ashes record. It also meant Waugh preserved a series average of 126.5.

Some thought that Border's late declaration may have cost us the match but in the end poor light saved England. Our game plan had not changed throughout the series, which was to bat England out of the game and then go for the throat. The West Indies had used the same tactics with great success and it served us well in this Ashes campaign.

Terry Alderman had taken five wickets for the sixth time in the series and became the first bowler to take 40 wickets in a series on more than one occasion. On this tour his 41 wickets included 19 lbw's which says a lot about bowling stump to stump.

1990 /1991

This was an extremely confident team that went into battle against England. Two Western Australian bowlers were the key. Terry Alderman, of the wicket-to-wicket bowling and late swing, and the languid giant Bruce Reid who had his spine rebuilt for the occasion.

1990/91 – BRISBANE – FIRST TEST
November 23, 24, 25
ENGLAND 194 *(Gower 61, Reid 4 for 53)* and 114 *(Alderman 6 for 47)*
AUSTRALIA 152 and 0 for 157 *(Marsh 72, Taylor 67)*
Australia won by 10 wickets

Fifteen months after The Oval debacle nothing had improved for England – or at least very little.

They were bundled out for 194 in the first innings with yet another elegant 61 from David Gower. The giant Bruce Reid, who had spent the last 18 months having his fragile back rebuilt with steel rods and screws, was the best of the attack taking four wickets.

Surprisingly we were little better and rolled for 152 in our visit to the crease.

Then it was England's turn to look foolish with the bat, and they did. Bowling under grey clouds, Alderman proceeded to his best Test figures of 6/47 to show the English that he could bowl just as well in Australia as he could on their home turf. It was the eleventh time he had taken five or more wickets in an innings, but the first time in Australia.

We needed 157 for victory and again there were knees knocking around the nation. However, Australia should not have worried. After the batting mayhem of the previous days, Mark Taylor and Geoff Marsh were unbroken when they gained the winning runs, again leaving me strapped to my pads in the dressing room.

1990/91 – MELBOURNE – SECOND TEST
December 26, 27, 28, 29, 30
ENGLAND 352 (*Gower 100, Stewart 79, Larkins 64, Reid 6 for 97*) and 150 (*Gooch 58, Larkins 54, Reid 7 for 51*)
AUSTRALIA 306 (*Border 62, Taylor 61, Jones 44, Fraser 6 for 82*) and 2 for 197 (*Boon 94, Marsh 79*)
Australia won by 8 wickets

As in Brisbane, England grabbed the initial break with a first innings lead but then suffered a disastrous second innings collapse to let us take the match.

Certainly England started well with yet another typical David Gower innings and for Australia the surgically rebuilt and realigned Reid proving an invaluable menace with six wickets.

We were again led by Mark Taylor and the stoic Allan Border with Dean Jones adding a touch of colour, scoring 44 runs off 57 balls.

For England the ungainly, hardworking and affable Angus Fraser took 6/82 with his medium quicks.

At 1/103, England looked solid but suddenly nine wickets fell for 47 runs including 6/3 immediately after tea.

Reid's performance of 7/51 gave him a remarkable 13 wickets for the match. Australia had slightly less than 200 as our target for victory and Geoff Marsh and I dutifully set about applying ourselves to the task during the final day of the match.

As we walked out to bat that morning I did my usual and wished "Swampy" Marsh the best of luck. He stared at me differently for an instant and said, "If you get out before we make these runs together I am going to kill you."

It was a partnership with my old mate that brings back the

fondest memories.

Our unbeaten 187 in five hours meant we had both passed 1,000 runs against England and had given Australia their second victory of the series.

Not since the 1890s had Australia won the first two Tests of a series after facing first innings deficits.

1990/91 – SYDNEY – THIRD TEST
January 4, 5, 6, 7, 8
AUSTRALIA 518 *(Matthews 128, Boon 97, Border 78, Jones 60, S. Waugh 48, Malcolm 4 for 128)* and 205 *(Healy 69, Tufnell 5 for 61)*
ENGLAND 8 for 469 declared *(Gower 123, Atherton 105, Stewart 91, Gooch 59)* and 4 for 113 *(Gooch 54).*
Match drawn

We were at ease as we stormed past 500 runs in our first innings. The highlight was undoubtedly a century by the highly unique Greg Matthews using borrowed equipment.

I paid the penalty for over exuberance when I hit three fours off an over from Graham Gooch and then was dismissed for attempting a fourth when on 97. Another 90 and yet another thwarted century against England. They were certainly adding up!

But England was not to be denied when it was their turn at the crease. Michael Atherton took control and his century was at a snail's pace 424 minutes which included only eight fours. In stark comparison Gower cracked eight boundaries in little more than half an hour while accompanying his slow-moving partner. Then Gooch surprisingly declared 49 runs behind. It was a master stroke as England knocked over Marsh and Taylor before stumps and on the final day were on

the attack and at full cry, but just could not pick up the required wickets.

Night watchman, Ian Healy stayed at the crease for almost three hours to top score with 69 while Carl Rackeman, also promoted up the order, created yet another record by taking 72 minutes to open his score. The two Queenslanders edged the score slowly upwards and in the end England had to make 255 off 28 overs to win.

Gooch and Gower had a slash as Border's face visibly darkened, but eventually the task was just too much.

Sydney was one of those special places for Boon and Marsh. Who says cricketers aren't superstitious. Before any game in Sydney we would walk through Martin Place, Centrepoint and then back to the hotel. On the way we would stop at the R.M. Williams shop where the lad from the back blocks of WA would touch all the clothing.

When asked if he would like some assistance he would reply, "No, I am just feeling some good luck."

After a few visits they recognised him and his odd behaviour and left us alone.

> **1990/91 – ADELAIDE – FOURTH TEST**
> *January 25, 26, 27, 28, 29*
> AUSTRALIA 386 (*M. Waugh 138, Matthews 65, Boon 49, McDermott 42, DeFreitas 4 for 56*) and 6 for 314 declared (*Boon 121, Border 83*)
> ENGLAND 229 (*Gooch 87, Smith 53, DeFreitas 45, McDermott 5 for 97, Reid 4 for 53*) and 5 for 335 (*Gooch 117, Atherton 87, Lamb 53*)
> **Match drawn**

This match heralded the arrival of Mark Waugh on the

Right: Brian Lara caught brilliantly by Boon bowled Steve Waugh in Antigua. Australia vs West Indies 1995.
Ray Titus Photography.

Test scene at the expense of his twin brother.

He immediately made his mark with an extremely stylish 138, which saw him lift Australia to 386.

He came into the dressing room at the end of his innings and said to AB, "What's so hard about this Test cricket. It's an easy game."

Craig McDermott, reinstated in the Test team after two years' absence, and the ever dangerous, when fit, Bruce Reid rolled England for 229 sharing nine wickets between them.

In the second innings Australia reigned supreme. Playing on one of my favourite Australian hunting grounds, I scored 121 and Border enjoyed the occasion with a vigorous 83 not out in contrast to many of his more battling innings.

Faced with more than 500 runs required for victory over an Australian team with three of our bowlers injured, Gooch and Atherton opened with a double century stand but the challenge was too much and the match was drawn.

1990/91 – PERTH – FIFTH TEST

February 1, 2, 3, 5
ENGLAND 244 *(Lamb 91, Smith 58, McDermott 8 for 97)* and 182 *(Smith 43, Newport 40, Hughes 4 for 37)*
AUSTRALIA 307 *(Boon 64, Matthews 60, Healy 42)* and 1 for 120 *(Marsh 63)*
Australia won by 9 wickets

On a fast Perth wicket, England could not cope with the speed blitz from Craig McDermott. The injury-prone Reid with 27 wickets in the series was rested, allegedly due to "calloused feet" but McDermott merely picked up his mantle and saw England collapse from 2/191 to be all out for 244 with the big red haired quick taking 8/97.

Border, leading Australia for a record 23rd time, was duly concerned with an early loss of wickets but then I managed a solid 64 and support from the tail saw us scramble to 307.

It gave me an aggregate of 530 for the series at an average of 75.71.

England then produced another typical trademark collapse losing 7/69 to the speed of Terry Alderman, Craig McDermott and Merv Hughes who shared the wickets.

It was Gooch's last Test against Australia and we hosted a farewell for him in our dressing room after the match. It didn't impress our irrepressible team manager Ian McDonald. No stranger to all night parties himself he let three senior players, including me, know exactly what he thought about the gesture.

1993

What a tour! The ball of the century from Shane Warne was the undoubted historical highlight. To see the bewildered look on Mike Gatting's face was priceless. Did that ball delight us? Yes, surprise us? Not really. His bowling in Sri Lanka a few weeks earlier had proved to us that the blond from Black Rock could bowl. We hadn't exactly been hiding him in the lead-up matches but we had not been over bowling him either.

From a personal perspective I had never made a century in an Ashes Test in England. Would that be how I was remembered? At Old Trafford I was tantalising close. Out for 93. I had been batting comfortably and had little cause for concern when an inside edge from Phillip DeFreitas somehow carried off my pad to Gatting at cover.

Angry, disappointed, stupid. All the emotions surged as I trudged back to the pavilion. Wham! I put my bat straight through the wicker cane chair as I commented on my dismissal. The room attendant, an old mate from my days at Lancashire

second XI, silently replaced the chair while AB quietly told me, "You will get it at Lord's next week."

Easy to say. Harder to achieve. Michel Slater and Matthew Hayden had been fighting run for run for the opener's booth and it ridiculously came down to the last preamble game. Slater made a century, Hayden a 90 – so Slater got the nod and belted 152 in his debut at Lord's. Cricket can be an oh so fickle game. Australia was well on top as I partnered Mark Waugh for 175 runs and then AB for 139.

My moment came when I scored a single off Chris Lewis to fine leg. The long wait was over. Not one for any over-the-top shows of celebration I controlled myself. But internally there was absolute elation with my first century in England, and at Lord's! Every time I return I still look with pride at the honour board and the names surrounding mine. "Not worthy" I think quietly to myself.

A century in England at the home of cricket. Of course Allan Border said, "I told you so." As I came back to the pavilion the members applauded and it was quite a feeling to walk up the same steps as W.G. Grace and Sir Donald Bradman after scoring a century. The ghosts of cricket had smiled on me that day.

By the time we reached Trent Bridge I was feeling very comfortable and in control of my game like never before. I managed another century and we got out of the match with a draw. Then Headingly and another century to help Australia take home the Ashes.

I had scored three centuries in three Tests. The first batsman since Don Bradman in 1938 to do so – a humbling experience.

1993 – OLD TRAFFORD – FIRST TEST

June 3, 4, 5, 6, 7

AUSTRALIA 289 (*Taylor 124, Slater 58, Such 6 for 67*) and 5 for 432 declared (*Healy 102, Boon 93, S. Waugh 78, M. Waugh 64*)

ENGLAND 210 (*Gooch 65, Warne 4 for 51, Hughes 4 for 59*) and 332 (*Gooch 133, Lewis 43, Warne 4 for 86, Hughes 4 for 92*)

Australia won by 179 runs

This was the memorable "ball of the century" match, which changed cricket history.

The game had started with Mark Taylor and debutant, Michael Slater, posting 128 for the first wicket but then we fell to the off-spin of Peter Such who finished with 6/67, the best by an English debutant against Australia since 1890.

Graham Gooch and Michael Atherton started with 71, and then came the ball which spun across Mike Gatting to clip the off stump, resulting in his expression of bewilderment and a flurry as history books were re-written.

No bowler in Ashes history had hit the stumps with their maiden ball and when Warne dismissed Robin Smith six balls later, Australia was on its way to victory.

I was at bat pad for the Gatting dismissal and just stared in amazement. History was made that day and I was touching distance from it.

Warne finished the match with eight wickets as did his fellow Victorian, Merv Hughes while I again missed a century, being tantalisingly close with 93 runs in the second innings.

The main thing is always the team but where was that elusive century?

1993 – LORD'S – SECOND TEST
June 17, 18, 19, 20, 21
AUSTRALIA 4 for 632 declared *(Boon 164, Slater 152, Taylor 111, M. Waugh 99, Border 77)*
ENGLAND 205 *(Atherton 80, Hughes 4 for 52, Warne 4 for 57)* and 365 *(Atherton 99, Hick 64, Stewart 62, Gatting 59, May 4 for 81, Warne 4 for 102)*
Australia won by an innings and 62 runs

Australia was supreme in this match, losing only four wickets to score our most decisive victory over the traditional foe.

New boy, Michael Slater, scored a superb 152 while, so tantalisingly close two weeks earlier, I scored my maiden Test century in England with an undefeated 164 at the home of cricket.

Mark Taylor also scored a century and Mark Waugh missed out by one run, destroying what could have been

the wonderful record of the top four batsmen all scoring centuries. England were now stumbling against Warne. He took four wickets in the first innings as did his big mate from Melbourne, Merv Hughes and then in the second, took another four to give Australia victory by an innings and 62 runs.

Playing what was to be his last game at Lord's, Border's 77 gave him an average of 100 at the famous ground. No wonder he liked playing there.

Australia's win was all the meritorious as the opening bowler, Craig McDermott had collapsed on the second evening of the match and returned to Australia after surgery for a twisted bowel.

1993 – TRENT BRIDGE – THIRD TEST
July 1, 2, 3, 5, 6
ENGLAND 321 *(Smith 86, Hussain 71, Hughes 5 for 92)* and 6 for 422 declared *(Gooch 120, Thorpe 114, Smith 50, Hussain 47)*
AUSTRALIA 373 *(Boon 101, M. Waugh 70, Slater 40, McCague 4 for 121)* and 6/202 *(Julian 56, S. Waugh 47)*
Match drawn

England began its fight back at Trent Bridge and its first innings score of 321 would have been greater if not for Merv Hughes, with the weight of the opening attack on his shoulders, taking his first five wicket haul against England.

We replied with 373 as I snared my fifth century against England, again sharing a century partnership with Mark Waugh. The cricket gods were smiling and the ball was looking as big as a soccer ball and my hand-eye co-ordination was never better.

England's second innings saw them appearing to master the spin of Warne, scoring more than 400 runs for the loss of only

six wickets, with Graham Gooch and Graham Thorpe leading the way.

Their resurgence might have been successful but for some stout resistance on the final afternoon of the match from Brendon Julian, now a television star on *Getaway*, and Steve Waugh. They combined for a partnership of 87 to frustrate the hosts.

1993 – HEADINGLY – FOURTH TEST
July 22, 23, 24, 25, 26
AUSTRALIA 4 for 653 declared *(Border 200, S. Waugh 157, Boon 107, Slater 67, M. Waugh 52)*
ENGLAND 200 *(Gooch 59, Atherton 55, Reiffel 5 for 65)* and 305 *(Stewart 78, Atherton 63, May 4 for 65)*
Australia won by an innings and 148 runs

Just how good was this Australian team? We retained the Ashes at Leeds with a victory that even outshone our Lord's win.

Again we lost only four wickets in the entire match and our 4 for 653 was the highest total of any match at Headingly.

Allan Border and Steve Waugh put on 332 without being separated which was the second highest in Test history. Border's 200 not out was his 26th Test century while my 107 was my 50th first class century and third in successive Ashes Tests – a similar performance to Don Bradman in 1938!

It also saw me pass 1,000 Test runs in England.

I have never felt more in control of my game. Shot selection, patience, execution and confidence were at their peak. I had never batted better.

England could manage only 200 in response with Warne strangely subdued. It was left to his Victorian team mate, Paul

Former Test fast bowler and Australian selector Merv Hughes remembers David Boon

Our Ashes tour in 1989 led to some long and solid celebrations. We started early after the First Test victory at Old Trafford ending the night at Pier 6. I can remember the name of the place, David Boon and not much else.

Boony disappeared to the urinal and while standing there contemplating the future of mankind thought he saw our off spinner Tim May walk in, face the bowl beside him and start fumbling to undo his trouser.

Knowing that Tim had consumed more than his fair share of celebrations Boon, ever helpful and multi-skilled, leaned over and with his spare hand started helping Tim with his trousers.

Unfortunately it was a total stranger.

Late in the 1989 Ashes Tour the wives were allowed to join us. Mrs Waugh, Mrs Jones and Mrs Boon arrived moving our manners up a notch.

Again after another big win we went on a sightseeing tour around the pubs and nightspots of London before deciding to settle down for dinner.

We ordered, they brought out entrée but when I looked around to ask Boony to pass the salt he had fallen head first into his food and was fast asleep. Lucky it wasn't soup or he could have drowned.

We could tell Mrs Boon was not impressed. Everyone in the restaurant could.

She woke him up and escorted him out of the restaurant – a well known place called Langons. Five minutes later Pip was back.

"I have given 20 pounds to a taxi driver and told him to get David safely to room 434 at the Westbury Hotel. He is not going to spoil my evening. I'm having too much fun."

Reiffel with 5/65 to do the damage.

Asked to follow-on, and after being booed from the field earlier, the English batsmen played with loose abandon to score 305 entertaining runs against the spin of Tim May, who took four wickets, but the deed was done and Australia won by an innings and 148 runs.

1993 – EDGBASTON – FIFTH TEST
August 5, 6, 7, 8, 9
ENGLAND 276 (*Atherton 72, Emburey 55, Stewart 45, Reiffel 6 for 71*) and 251 (*Thorpe 60, Gooch 48, Warne 5 for 82, May 5 for 89*)
AUSTRALIA 408 (*M. Waugh 137, Healy 80, S. Waugh 59*) and 2 for 120 (*M. Waugh 62*)
Australia won by 8 wickets

With the resignation of GrahamGooch the unflappable Michael Atherton became the youngest man to captain England at home against Australia and immediately played a long, steady innings to guide his team. Again his batsmen let him down falling to Paul Reiffel who took six wickets as England struggled to 276.

In reply the spin of Peter Such and John Emburey worried us. But after Steve Waugh survived a stumping chance he went on to score 153 in partnership with his twin brother, who scored a stylish century and guided Australia past 400 runs.

On the Sunday of the match it was time for Warne to rediscover his form.

He took three wickets and in another memorable performance bowled Gooch behind his legs with a huge leg break that transfixed cricket fans around the world. Off spinner Emburey, now 40 years of age, had batted stoutly in the

first innings for 55 not out and again showed almost solitary resistance making 47 in the second innings in more than three hours. He had batted for six hours in the match for his stoic 92 runs.

The eventual target was 120 and with grey skies and rain looming on the final day, there was nervousness in the Australian camp. Both openers fell to spin but then Mark Waugh and I again constructed a century stand, our fifth during the series, to guide our nation to victory.

1993 – THE OVAL – SIXTH TEST
August 19, 20, 21, 22, 23
ENGLAND 380 *(Hick 80, Stewart 76, Gooch 56, Atherton 50)* and 313 *(Gooch 79, Ramprakash 64, Atherton 42)*
AUSTRALIA 303 *(Healy 83, Taylor 70, Border 48, Fraser 5 for 87)* and 229 *(Reiffel 42, M. Waugh 40, Watkin 4 for 65)*
England won by 161 runs

England scored its first Ashes victory for seven years to the relief of the nation's cricket fans.

In the first innings England seemed to be desperate to reclaim some prestige from the series. All the batsmen got runs with Graeme Hick top scoring with 80. In fact they combined to score 59 boundaries on the first day. In response Australia's batsmen didn't have their minds on the job and but for an undefeated 83 from wicket-keeper, Ian Healy, would have mustered a very ordinary score against the medium pace of Angus Fraser.

Again, England scored more than 300 in their second innings and Australia with its batsmen gone missing again, scored only 229 to give England victory by 161 runs.

Hughes, by now limping, sore and obviously a walking wounded, finished the series with 31 wickets while Warne took

34 off more than 400 overs to ignite the imagination of cricket fans around the world.

My respect for Merv was immense. He had carried the Australian fast bowling attack after the departure of McDermott. On the outside he appeared the same, but in fact he was all pain and soreness. Surgery was required on all parts of the big fella's body when he returned to Australia.

But not to his heart. Nothing wrong there.

1994/1995

The Melbourne Test was undoubtedly the highlight. Shane Warne taking six wickets in the first innings, my 20th Test century and then Warne's hat trick, with me playing a role. Fantastic!

1994/95 – BRISBANE – FIRST TEST

November 25, 26, 27, 28, 29
AUSTRALIA 426 (*Slater 176, M. Waugh 140, Taylor 59, Gough 4 for 107*) and 8 for 248 declared (*Taylor 58, Slater 45, Healy 45, Tufnell 4 for 79*)
ENGLAND 167 (*Atherton 54, McDermott 6 for 53*) and 323 (*Hick 80, Thorpe 67, Gooch 56, Warne 8 for 71*)
Australia won by 184 runs

We were determined to cause England instant pain when we gathered for the First Test in Brisbane in November 1994.

It began with openers Mark Taylor and Michael Slater compiling an opening partnership of 99 which cleared the way for Mark Waugh with all his elegant stroke play to join the ever audacious Slater.

It was wonderful cricket and they scored 182 runs in two and a half hours as Slater made a massive 176, scoring 100 of

174

Right: Last Test 100. Australia vs Sri Lanka, MCG 1996.

those runs in boundaries. The Aussies totalled 426 and it looked even larger by stumps with England at 6/133 in reply. The rout continued the next day with Craig McDermott finishing with 6/53 and England seemingly at Australia's mercy.

Surprisingly to some, but not to me, Taylor did not enforce the follow-on, preferring to have Warne bowl last on a wicket that showed promise for spinners.

Taylor and Slater again had a century opening stand but then Australia lost 8/92, forcing Taylor to finally declare at 8/248.

Phil Tufnell took four wickets which only fuelled the flames around the Warne mystique – just how many he would take on this wicket.

Survival was not beyond the imagination of the English at stumps on day four with their score 2/211. But then Warne took the ball. The English had decided on a bat pad resistance but it was for nought.

Three wickets in four balls broke the back of the innings and the leg spinner finished with 8/71 for the innings and 11 wickets for the match.

1994/95 – MELBOURNE – SECOND TEST
December 24, 26, 27, 28, 29
AUSTRALIA 279 *(S. Waugh 94, M. Waugh 71, Boon 41, Gough 4 for 60)* and 7 for 320 declared *(Boon 131, Slater 44)*
ENGLAND 212 *(Thorpe 51, Atherton 44, Warne 6 for 64)* and 92 *(McDermott 5 for 42)*
Australia won by 295 runs

If England had been unlucky in the First Test then they were cursed in the second. Three questionable umpiring decisions went against them and wicket-keeper, Alec Stewart's

index finger was broken by Craig McDermott.

We had struggled on a damp wicket with only the Waugh twins being able to handle the situation with any authority. I scored a struggling 41 against some hostile bowling from Darren Gough.

In response England started well but then Warne struck, taking 6/64 to give his team a 67 run lead on the first innings. On the fourth day I got going although Darren Gough and Phil Tufnell caused me some concern. I went on to my 20th century and seventh against England. I played some strong shots through the arc from mid-off to mid-on and my footwork was back to its twinkling best – well, they were moving again.

England was set 388 in four sessions but when Damien Fleming broke through twice before stumps they fell to 4/79. Then the last six wickets collapsed for 13 runs with Warne performing the first Ashes hat trick (Phillip DeFreitas, Gough and Devon Malcolm) since Hugh Trumble, also at the MCG, almost a century earlier. I played my part taking DeFreitas at bat pad to give Warne the third dismissal and the hat trick.

What a thrill to be part of a hat trick. And it all happened on my birthday. The catch featured on the front page of *The Herald-Sun* and Shane wrote a very nice piece about it. Another one of those cricket memories you will never forget.

We had expected a long day in the field. Yet within an hour we were pulling corks out of champagne bottles and toasting yet another resounding result.

177

1994/95 – SYDNEY –THIRD TEST
January 1, 2, 3, 4, 5
ENGLAND 309 *(Atherton 88, Crawley 72, Gough 51, McDermott 5 for 101)* and 2 for 255 declared *(Hick 98, Atherton 67, Thorpe 47)*
AUSTRALIA 116 *(Taylor 49, Gough 6 for 4)* and 7 for 344 *(Taylor 113, Slater 103, Fraser 5 for 73)*
Match drawn

Everyone thought England would be in disarray after the Melbourne Test but there was plenty of fight and fortitude in the British lion.

England lost Graham Gooch, Graeme Hick and Graham Thorpe with only 20 runs on the board but then Michael Atherton and John Crawley put on 174 in a five hour face-saving stand. Craig McDermott on and off the field with illness, chipped in for wickets as each side pushed for an advantage.

Darren Gough scored a whirlwind 50 and even Angus Fraser made 27 over two laborious hours which frustrated the Australian bowlers.

Rain then affected the match and we went to bat losing three quick wickets for 18 and then being 8/65. Australia looked certain to have to face the follow-on but Mark Taylor scratched around for an unconvincing 49 in a stand with McDermott off 51. This saved the day against a rampaging Gough who finished with 6/49.

With rain still interfering, Atherton, Thorpe and Hick went about establishing a score for Australia to chase.

Hick was only two runs away from a century when his captain declared leaving the batsman stunned and the captain

claiming that he was "dawdling" after being told what time the skipper wanted to close the innings.

Needing 449 to win, Australia raced to 208 at lunch on the final day with both Michael Slater and Mark Taylor making centuries and England again getting no assistance from the umpires.

Then Australia slid to 7/292 in a manner reminiscent of our darkest era.

On a helpful wicket Angus Fraser, who had been called up from Sydney grade cricket, was sometimes unplayable.

Tim May joined Warne on the fall of the seventh wicket with 18 overs remaining. The pair survived in gloomy light for 77 minutes. Tufnell tried all he knew but the Australian spin bowlers survived.

1994/95 – ADELAIDE – FOURTH TEST
January 26, 27, 28, 29, 30
ENGLAND 353 *(Gatting 117, Atherton 80, Gooch 47)* and 328 *(DeFreitas 88, Thorpe 83, Crawley 71, M. Waugh 5 for 40)*
AUSTRALIA 419 *(Blewett 102, Taylor 90, Healy 74, Slater 67)* and 156 *(Healy 51, Lewis 4 for 24, Malcolm 4 for 39)*
England won by 106 runs

Warne had taken only one wicket in Sydney despite taking 20 in the first two matches and England's batting resurgence had given the visitors some hope. It was reflected in their performance in Adelaide when they scored 353 led by the sterling performance of Mike Gatting. It was his first Test century for seven and a half years and took 411 minutes, but it set the scene for the Test match.

However, Australia was not to be denied the batting honours and with newcomer Greg Blewett, scoring an

undefeated 102, and Taylor, falling tantalisingly 10 runs short of another century managed to give Australia a first innings lead. Blewett, a 23-year-old South Australian became the 18th Australian batsman to score a century on debut against England and, as the tail collapsed, had to rely on fellow debutant, Peter McIntyre to stay around to achieve his hundred.

Gatting made a duck as England lost two wickets before wiping off the small 25 run arrears.

Thorpe and Crawley scored well but it was the bowler and sometimes all-rounder, DeFreitas, who set Australia back on our heels scoring 88 off 95 balls including 22 off a McDermott over.

Our recognised bowlers went missing leaving Mark Waugh to secure his first five wicket Test haul. Australia was faced with the task of making 263 off 67 overs – a not insurmountable total.

However, we were soon in trouble at 4/23 when Lewis, who the previous week had been playing club cricket in Melbourne, dismissed McDermott. Australia was 8/83 and it was left to Healy to again lead a stout defence. But to no avail as England won with 35 balls to spare.

1994/95 – PERTH – FIFTH TEST
February 3, 4, 5, 6, 7
AUSTRALIA 402 *(Slater 124, S. Waugh 99, M. Waugh 88)* and 8 for 345 declared *(Blewett 115, S. Waugh 80, Taylor 52, Slater 45)*
ENGLAND 295 *(Thorpe 123, Ramprakash 72, Lewis 40)* and 123 *(Ramprakash 42, McDermott 6 for 38)*
Australia won by 329 runs

Australia's 402 was established by Slater, yet again, and

185

strokemakers. His game was characterised by an ability to drive, cut, pull and loft the ball so effortlessly that it could make him look disdainful of the talents of bowlers.

I remember his gifted 138 on Test debut, three commanding centuries as an opener at the 1996 World Cup tournament and his 126 to seal the Frank Worrell Trophy in West Indies in 1995.

Next Allan Border. I had the honour of batting with him on many occasions. As has been said so often, if you wanted someone to bat for your life then he was your man.

Steve Waugh wasn't far behind him as far as grit and determination was concerned. Who can forget that century in Sydney? Batting at the fall of the fourth wicket he could give a team accelerated run-making or battle it out with the tail-end like no other.

Behind the stumps and batting next is Ian Healy. He won matches for Australia with bat and gloves.

Adam Gilchrist fans will be in uproar but remember I never played with him. Certainly Gilly is an amazing batsman – but Healy was no slouch either.

But the silky glovework of the Queenslander was superb, especially to Shane Warne.

Gilchrist is constantly improving in this area and will undoubtedly become the equal of Healy over the next 12 months. At that stage I will revisit my selection.

Warne selects himself. Who could argue that he is not the greatest spin bowler of all time? Enough said.

Now for the rabbits with the bat and tigers with the ball.

My opening attack is Glenn McGrath and Bruce Reid. Supporting them is the huge-hearted Merv Hughes edging out Craig McDermott.

Why Bruce Reid? Wasn't he merely a meteor across the

cricket sky? He made his debut in the same match as Merv and Geoff Marsh when Australia was at its lowest ebb.

Tall, gangly Reid was a left arm bowler with a steep bounce who could magically slant the ball away. He was the mainstay of our attack but we never saw enough of him. His slight frame continually broke down and his back was rebuilt with steel rods and aluminium screws.

His finest moment came when he took 13 wickets against England at the MCG in 1990/91. A year later he was finished.

Merv Hughes rarely broke down or let you down. If you wanted Allan Border to bat for you then you wanted Merv to bowl for you.

He often carried the Australian attack and lifted himself to Herculean performances while others fell around him. More than 200 Test scalps against some of the best batting teams in the world.

Merv is "must" for my team.

As for 12th man then its either Dean Jones, Tim May or Craig McDermott – all of whom will be furious with me because I didn't squeeze them into the team.

World XI

What a surfeit of talent when considering a world team.

For openers I have vivid and painful memories of Gordon Greenidge and Desmond Haynes.

This legendary pair came together for the first time in a Test in 1978. West Indies was playing Australia at Queen's Park Oval, Trinidad and in their first outing they came up with a partnership of 87 runs – only three runs less than Australia's first innings score.

Over the next 12 years the two Barbadians carved a

niche for themselves in cricket history as the best performed partnerships of all time. They batted against bowlers like Dennis Lillee, Richard Hadlee, Jeff Thomson, Imran Khan and Kapil Dev to notch up 15 century partnerships.

In 89 Tests they averaged 44.07.

They opened the innings for West Indies in 102 One-Day internationals and featured in partnerships worth 5,150 runs at an average of 52.55 per innings.

Fans of Sunil Gavaskar will be reaching for their *Wisdens* but I just didn't see enough of him.

The other batsmen pick themselves.

Vivian Richards, Sachin Tendulkar and Brian Lara.

That trio kept David Gower out of my team. What more can you say.

Next is my old mate Ian Botham. Selected as an all rounder he could just about make the team as a batsman – or a bowler. With bat or ball nothing was beyond him. As Australia continually discovered.

I have given the gloves to West Indian Jeffrey Dujon who made 270 dismissals behind the stumps and "enjoyed" keeping to the world's greatest array of fast bowlers. He could turn half chances into catches and his leg side work was outstanding.

But who will he keep to in this match?

Malcolm Marshall will open the bowling with Richard Hadlee. Wasim Akram and Curtly Ambrose will support them.

Fans of Joel Garner, Michael Holding and Allan Donald will be rightly upset. I only played against Holding on a couple of occasions – anyway who would you push out of the team for these four?

Marshall had all the toys and knew how to use them. He slid to the wicket but he was quick, damn quick. He wasn't tall but he had a bouncer as mean as anyone's and a leg cutter that

189

cleaned me up on a few occasions. He was the best of the lot. Sadly he died of cancer in 1999 aged 41.

Richard Hadlee, the nemesis of Australia, will open at the other end. Cool and calculating Richard Hadlee was cricket's silent assassin.

He was the first man to take 400 Test wickets with his forensically accurate seam and swing. Australian crowds had a love –hate relationship with him and so did the Aussie cricketers. We loved to hate him.

But he was good, very, very good. A perfect foil for the outlandish speed of Marshall and Ambrose.

Wasim Akram was another not loved by the crowds but more than 400 Test wickets and 500 in One-Day matches ranks him with the greats of the game.

Such a rich array of speed means there is no spin bowler, perhaps John Emburey or Abdul Qadir can carry the drinks. Sorry fellows!

Issues Facing Cricket

The greatest challenge facing Australian cricket is remaining diligent. We are the world's foremost cricketing nation (ignore the loss of the Ashes) but to retain the stature we must not ease back on our achievements. We must continually promote cricket and through the excellent pathways now established seek out young players and give them the advantage of attending the Centre of Excellence in Queensland.

When appropriate we will require players capable of replacing State players when they retire and of course Test players when they come to the end of their playing days.

Selectors

Australian selectors were once anonymous blokes in suits.

Now we always seem to be in the public eye. Previous Chairman Trevor Hohns who guided Australia to the peak of world cricket has retired, and Andrew Hilditch is in the chair.

Allan Border is back as a selector. Then of course there is Merv Hughes and the stumpy chap from Tasmania.

What is Hilditch like? Will our policy on selection be different under our new boss?

Andrew Hilditch is conservative. Certainly no radical in dark pin striped suit and spotted tie type. I suspect the change of chairman will be seamless and smooth.

The consensus style of selection will continue. We will continue to talk our way through selections and continue to seek Ricky Ponting's input.

Importantly we will continue to keep players abreast of our thinking on where we see them and their future. There will be no surprises for the players!

The selectors will pick the best team on each occasion. Age will not be a consideration. There is no opportunity for investing in youth or gambling on a wildcard.

Certainly retirements may be pending but younger players will have to force their way into the team. We will not be offering anyone an early exit in order to give youth a go unless it is really justified!

There will be opportunities – but will they occur during an Ashes Series?

Our challenge will be player maintenance. Making the best use of them for longer. Over the next few years we will need to measure their workload in order to maximise the benefit to Australia and the player!

Allan Border, my favourite all-time player and captain is back as a selector. His knowledge of the game, and more importantly, the players will be fantastic.

If we can just stop Merv Hughes from putting his tongue in everyone's ear whenever there is a wicket, I think we can get on very well! By the way, ignore the tom foolery, Merv is very knowledgeable about cricket.

Have and Have Not

Plenty has been written about the gap between the cricketing nations of the world. The quality of everything from pitches and coaching to sponsorship and general support for countries like England and Australia compared to Bangladesh and Zimbabwe.

We have invited them into the cricket family and we cannot afford to ignore them. We must embrace and assist them if cricket is to grow as an international sport and not be regarded as a hangover from a previous empire.

Anyway the gap is closing as these "minnows" are increasingly offered the opportunity to play at international level. The "Top End" cricket through Darwin and Cairns has been a revelation which will continue, and continue to bring tremendous benefits.

Scheduling

Only one Test playing nation is located in the northern hemisphere and so the pressures on the southern summer – October to March – are horrendous.

Will we ever lose our traditional MCG Boxing Day Test match to South Africa to placate claims that the ICC should be even-handed in their scheduling? Not when you can attract 80,000 fans to the ground and a financial bonanza for Cricket Australia and for cricket generally.

Career Statistics Bowling

	Tests	ODI	First Class
Balls	36	82	1153
Runs	14	86	969
Wickets	0	0	14
Average	–	–	49.71
Economy	2.33	9.29	3.62

Born: December 29, 1960, Launceston, Tasmania.

Debut for Tasmania: December 10, 1978.

Gillette Cup Final Victory for Tasmania: January 14, 1979.

Married: Pip Wright April 30, 1983.

Prime Minister's XI, January 12 1984 V West Indies (Scored 134 off 136 balls)

One-Day debut: February 12, 1984

Test Debut: November 23, 1984

Appointed Vice Captain of Australia: August 14, 1986

Georgina Boon Born: April 7, 1988

Jack Boon Born: June 12, 1991

Father Clarrie Dies: February 12, 1993

Elizabeth Boon Born: February 3, 1995

Last One-Day Game: March 15, 1995.

Test career finishes: Sunday January 29, 1996 Adelaide as Australia defeats Sri Lanka 3-0.

Write to Boony

Now it's your turn at the crease. Send me your favorite and worst cricket jokes, yarns, stunts, anecdotes, tragedies and victories.

As you can tell, I love reading and collecting these. Not just about the big time Test stars but about cricket and life everywhere. Your best and worst Boony doll tales too.

A selection just might make it to my next book. With suitable acknowledgement. So you too can be a literary legend.

Send to:
ken.davis@cliftongroup.com.au

Everyone knows I enjoy a beer. Always have with my mates and family. No way it knocks me for six. I love life too much. Responsible drinking. That's the way after a good innings. I reckon I've earned one now with mate and co-author, Ken Davis.

Cheers!

Yours In Cricket – Boony